Mac OS X
Leopard

P H R A S E B O O K

ESSENTIAL CODE AND COMMANDS

Brian Tiemann

**DEVELOPER'S
LIBRARY**

800 East 96th Street, Indianapolis, Indiana 46240 USA

Mac OS X Leopard Phrasebook

Copyright © 2008 by Pearson Education

All rights reserved. No part of this book shall be reproduced, stored in a retrieval system, or transmitted by any means, electronic, mechanical, photocopying, recording, or otherwise, without written permission from the publisher. No patent liability is assumed with respect to the use of the information contained herein. Although every precaution has been taken in the preparation of this book, the publisher and author assume no responsibility for errors or omissions. Nor is any liability assumed for damages resulting from the use of the information contained herein.

ISBN-10: 0-672-32954-9

ISBN-13: 978-0-672-32954-8

Library of Congress Cataloging-in-Publication Data

Tiemann, Brian.

    Mac OS X Leopard phrasebook / Brian Tiemann.

        p. cm.

    Includes index.

    ISBN 978-0-672-32954-8 (pbk.)

1. Mac OS. 2. UNIX (Computer file) 3. Operating systems (Computers) 4. Macintosh (Computer)–Programming. I. Title.

QA76.76.063T5745 2008

005.4'32–dc22   2007042738

Printed in the United States of America

First Printing: November 2007

Trademarks

All terms mentioned in this book that are known to be trademarks or service marks have been appropriately capitalized. Pearson cannot attest to the accuracy of this information. Use of a term in this book should not be regarded as affecting the validity of any trademark or service mark.

Warning and Disclaimer

Every effort has been made to make this book as complete and as accurate as possible, but no warranty or fitness is implied. The information provided is on an "as is" basis. The author and the publisher shall have neither liability nor responsibility to any person or entity with respect to any loss or damages arising from the information contained in this book.

Bulk Sales

Pearson offers excellent discounts on this book when ordered in quantity for bulk purchases or special sales. For more information, please contact

    U.S. Corporate and Government Sales

    1-800-382-3419   corpsales@pearsontechgroup.com

For sales outside of the U.S., please contact

    International Sales

    international@pearsoned.com

Acquisitions Editor	**Copy Editor**	**Technical Editor**	**Page Layout**
Mark Taber	Barbara Hacha	John Ray	TexTech, Inc.
Managing Editor	**Indexer**	**Publishing Coordinator**	
Patrick Kanouse	Ken Johnson	Vanessa Evans	
Project Editor	**Proofreader**	**Book Designer**	
Seth Kerney	Water Crest Publishing, Inc.	Gary Adair	

Contents at a Glance

Table of Contents

About the Author

Brian Tiemann is a freelance technology columnist and software engineer who has operated his own business and leisure websites on servers running BSD—the technology underlying Mac OS X—since 1995. As an outspoken advocate for the Apple Macintosh platform as well as for FreeBSD, he values a synthesis between open-source and closed-source development and believes FreeBSD and Mac OS X both validate that synthesis for the benefit of all users. He resides in San Jose, is a graduate of Caltech, and is the author of *Mac OS X Tiger in a Snap* and *FreeBSD Unleashed*.

We Want to Hear from You!

As the reader of this book, *you* are our most important critic and commentator. We value your opinion and want to know what we're doing right, what we could do better, what areas you'd like to see us publish in, and any other words of wisdom you're willing to pass our way.

You can email or write me directly to let me know what you did or didn't like about this book—as well as what we can do to make our books stronger.

Please note that I cannot help you with technical problems related to the topic of this book, and that due to the high volume of mail I receive, I might not be able to reply to every message.

When you write, please be sure to include this book's title and author as well as your name and phone or email address. I will carefully review your comments and share them with the author and editors who worked on the book.

Email: opensource@samspublishing.com

Mail: Mark Taber
        Associate Publisher
        Sams Publishing
        800 East 96th Street
        Indianapolis, IN 46240 USA

Reader Services

Visit our website and register this book at **www. samspublishing.com/register** for convenient access to any updates, downloads, or errata that might be available for this book.

Introduction

When then-Apple-CEO Gil Amelio announced in 1997 that the company had bought NeXT and that Steve Jobs, Apple's erstwhile founder and visionary, would be returning, many die-hard Macintosh fans were horrified. Apple was not in good shape at the time, and the purchase of NeXT almost certainly meant that the beloved but creaky old Mac OS would be replaced by something new: the rock-solid but rather schizophrenic NeXTSTEP/OPENSTEP operating system developed at Jobs's company. This operating system was based on Unix and aimed at high-powered professional workstation users, not the novices and creative pros who traditionally used Macs. To many, then, the absorption of NeXT meant the imminent end of the era of the Macintosh as the user-friendly, nonthreatening computer for everyday people.

All eyes were on Jobs as he took control and began rebuilding Apple from its mid-90s doldrums, and nobody was quite sure what to expect from the rumored next-generation operating system, code named Rhapsody, which was being built for Macintosh computers mostly by Jobs's long-time collaborators from NeXT. Would Rhapsody be just like the old Mac OS, with the old, well-worn look and feel, but more stable? Or would it be more like OPENSTEP—an often too-thin veneer of usability over an awkward and hard-edged core of Unix?

As it turned out, the Mac OS X that Apple shipped to customers in 2001 had genes from both of its progenitors. From the user's standpoint, it shared most of its design metaphors with the classic Mac OS, and a long-time Mac user could figure it out without too much trouble. But under the hood, it was a NeXT fan's dream; without putting too fine a point on it, Mac OS X is really the most modern version of OPENSTEP, with a flashy user interface and some libraries for classic Mac OS compatibility tacked on. Programmers used to the NeXT way of doing things hardly had to change a thing; Apple's Xcode is essentially the same development kit used at NeXT throughout the 1990s. Apple's creation of the slick Aqua interface, with its transparency and animation effects, went a long way toward making this system friendly to the casual user, but there were inevitably a lot of things that novices had to get used to, such as multiuser operation, Unix permissions, and the occasional need—especially toward the beginning, when a lot of features had not yet been fully implemented— to open up this spooky thing called the Terminal where textual Unix commands were to be typed.

Don't get me wrong. Very little in Mac OS X *requires* you to know how to operate the Terminal, the window into the computer's engine compartment. In Apple's design philosophy, everything the typical user needs is provided in the friendly graphical environment where commands can be picked from a translucent menu using a mouse with a drop-shadowed pointer. (Even the Terminal itself, as you'll see in Chapter 2, "Configuring Your Terminal," has drop shadows and can be configured to be transparent to whatever degree you want.) But Apple's design traditions also dictate that whatever the nontypical user needs to do is a bit harder to find: not impossible, but hidden away so those more esoteric functions don't get in the way of what the novices need. That's where the Terminal and the Unix environment it opens up come into play.

That's the purpose of this book: to unravel the mysteries of the Terminal, to give you the tools you need to accomplish things not accounted for in Mac OS X's basic feature set, and to introduce some perhaps quicker and more efficient ways to do things that the Aqua GUI already lets you do. It might not be so pretty in Terminal-land—but to a Unix-head, there's nothing quite so beautiful as a textual command line.

Audience for This Book

Go to any Linux Expo or BSD Conference in this day and age, and you'll notice something about the laptops the attendees are carrying around. The vast majority of them have glowing Apple logos on them. PowerBooks and MacBook Pros are far and away the preferred tools of the trade for those engaged in the world of cross-platform and open-source software development. It's not just because now that Apple has shifted its product line to Intel hardware, a Mac can run native versions of Windows, FreeBSD, and Linux, allowing the user to swap between worlds as needed. It's also because Mac OS X is itself a very capable Unix, with an open-source architecture (called Darwin) that anybody in the community can contribute to, and which can be used to run all the open-source software developed for the burgeoning Linux community, all within the auspices of the lickable, candy-like Aqua interface.

The audience for a book about the Terminal and the more esoteric tricks of working with Mac OS X is by necessity not a novice one. This book is supposed to be small enough to fit in a back pocket, and so it's meant for those Mac users who are familiar enough with getting around Mac OS X that there's no need for me to explain what the Dock is or how to open up the System Preferences. Likewise, if we're assuming that you're the kind of reader who has a genuine need to use the Terminal, you're probably already more or less familiar with Unix, and so we'll go light on the really hard-core Unix shell tricks such as pipes, output processing, and shell programming. You're here to learn how Mac OS X interacts with the Unix architecture you already know, not to study the intricate details of Unix itself, which you can get more efficiently from a bigger book more specifically dedicated to Unix or Linux. Mac OS X may be the most widely deployed and used Unix in the world, but it's still a Mac first and foremost, and there are plenty of tips and tricks to cover just in the Aqua interface.

The title of this book may be *Mac OS X Leopard Phrasebook*, but I'm thinking of it more like a traveler's guide. It's not enough to know how to speak the language in an unfamiliar city, and sometimes even the language is unimportant compared with simply knowing where to go and how to get there. Thus, this book isn't so much about the mysterious incantations described in other books in the *Phrasebook* series. Rather, it's intended to help you make the most of your experience as a Mac user, whether you're a Windows or Linux geek just getting your feet wet in an unfamiliar environment that you feel you ought to be able to instinctively grok better, or whether you're a long-time Mac-head who's never really reached beyond the limits of what Apple has made easily available to the casual user. Either way, with the help of this book, you should be able to dig deeper and with more sure-footedness into the capabilities of your computer than you had before.

Conventions Used in This Book

This book uses the following conventions:

- Monospace type is used to indicate commands, code, or text that appears in program output within the command-line Terminal environment. For example, the df command is referred to in monospace type, as are its command-line options (such as -h or --human-readable). Output from the command might look like this:

```
Filesystem                    512-blocks      Used
➡Avail Capacity  Mounted on
/dev/disk0s9                   490194432 368805376
➡120877056   75%    /
devfs                                               208
➡208        0   100%   /dev
```

- As in the df example, you'll also find continuation arrows (➡) at the beginning of certain lines of text. This means that the text is too long to be printed on a single line in the book, but it is actually supposed to be interpreted as a single continuous line. In other words, if you see a command line that spans two or more lines printed in the book, and there are continuation arrows at the beginnings of the lines beyond the first one, don't press Return at the end of the first line, in the middle of the command—just keep typing the whole thing, and then press Return at the very end.

- `Bold` monospaced text is used to indicate command text that you type yourself, in contrast to program output or textual prompts.

- **Bold** proportional text is used to indicate commands that you select from menus in the graphical Mac OS X interface.

- *Italic* monospaced text is used to indicate replacement text—a portion of a command or program output that is supposed to be replaced by text that you supply. For instance, `ls` *`foldername`* is a command that lets you supply any folder name you want—for instance, `ls` `Desktop`.

- You'll also find the following elements, which are used to introduce pertinent information related to the main subjects being covered:

NOTE: A Note presents interesting pieces of information related to the surrounding discussion.

TIP: A Tip offers advice or teaches an easier way to do something.

CAUTION: A Caution advises you about potential problems and helps you steer clear of disaster.

## 1

The Structure of Mac OS X

The Mac, first and foremost, is a computer designed—
as the ads used to say—"for the rest of us," meaning
those of us who aren't so technologically inclined as to
dream in C++ code and write our own device drivers
for the mysterious gadgets we pick up from yard sales
at houses with bats flying in and out of upstairs windows. That generally means that the user experience
of the Mac is intentionally limited only to those functions that the average, casual, novice computer user
might require of it. It's a mistake, however, to think
that the shiny, colorful buttons and menus you see in
the translucent Aqua interface represent all there is to
the Mac. There's more—far more—under the hood;
just because you don't see it immediately doesn't mean
it's not there. Between the slick Aqua layer and the
muscle-bound Unix layer underneath, it's a real Jekyll-
and-Hyde act that the operating system performs.

Using Mac OS X effectively means being able to
harness both sides of its split personality. This chapter
discusses how Mac OS X is structured, why it's divided
between the graphical and command-line layers, and

why it's useful to know how to operate in both environments if you want to get the most out of your Mac.

There won't be any commands in this chapter—just an overview of how the system is put together so that the commands you'll see later make sense.

Two Operating Systems in One

If you could dissect your Mac's operating system software and lay it all out on a table, you'd see that very little space is taken up by what we might call the "skin"—the polished Aqua interface that gives us access to our file icons, folders, menus, and utilities such as the Dock. Aqua is a layer that sits at the very top of the architecture of the system, draped over it like a drop cloth, hiding a lot of messy and ugly stuff from view.

If you're coming from a Linux or Unix background, the Aqua interface is analogous to KDE, GNOME, or any of the other window managers you might be used to—and just as superfluous to the work you might be used to doing, if the command line is your natural home. Without Aqua, you'd be missing all the carefully engineered graphical functions that Apple is so famous for. But most of the operating system, and most of its key functionality, is all still there: its kernel (the central process of the system, the one that deals directly with device drivers and the TCP/IP networking stack and coordinates the operation of all the applications you run), the filesystem, the disks, the networking subsystem, and all the other things that compose a computer that may or may not even have a monitor hooked up to it. Darwin, like all Unixes, is designed first and foremost to be equally usable from any terminal, whether local or remote, whether textual or graphical. You can log in to the system from halfway around the world, using only a lightweight text terminal that displays 25 rows of alphanumeric characters by 80 characters per row, and (with a few exceptions, such as user and group management) you can still have as much control over the core functions of the Mac OS X operating system as if you were sitting right in front of the computer.

NOTE: Rather than Aqua, it's perhaps more accurate to describe the Quartz compositing layer, which is based on Adobe's PDF standard, as being analogous to KDE or GNOME. Aqua is really just the specific "skin" Apple has applied to the Quartz display layer. Nonetheless, throughout this book I'll use "Aqua" to refer to the graphical user interface in Mac OS X in a general sense.

It would, however, be a mistake to think of the Aqua layer as unimportant. This is, after all, a Mac; if you just wanted a command-line Unix computer, you could have installed Linux or FreeBSD on a cheap PC and had all the Unix goodness you could handle. But no— you bought a Mac because, although its Unix under-pinnings are a nice bonus, the real magic happens in the graphical layer. There are things you can do with a mouse and a menu system and multiple layered win-dows that just aren't possible at the command line: copying and pasting data from one application to another, selecting whole groups of files visually and dragging them from one place to another, exploring all the possibilities of an application's functionality just by poking around in the menus, and a whole lot more.

The vast majority of the applications that you can buy or download for the Mac are graphical, designed to run in the Aqua interface; this is in contrast to the Linux world, where most programs are geared for the command line. In this sense, the Mac is defined by the Aqua environment and the applications you run within it, and hardly anyone ever thinks about the Unix underneath it. But if you have the need for more than what a lineup of graphical applications can offer you—if you're in the market for the flexibility and portability of Unix—buying a Mac means getting two complete operating systems for the price of one.

NOTE: Windows has a somewhat similar architecture to Mac OS X, in that there's a graphical layer in which most users spend all their time, and there's also an MS-DOS window that you can fire up to run the batch files and network troubleshooting commands that are still an inevitable part of the modern computing world, especially if you use applications like Oracle or other big-iron databases that are manipulated by SQL scripts and batch programs. However, the MS-DOS shell in Windows is really a tiny program with minimal functionality compared to the full Unix environment that comes with Mac OS X.

Uses for the Command Line

The heart and soul of the Mac is what you can do with it visually. Remember, Apple's original insight that made it a powerhouse of personal computer design back in the 80s was that people can operate more efficiently using the human brain's natural tendency to remember objects by their spatial placement, color, movement, and other visual characteristics, not by their names, dates of last modification, permissions, or the rest of the abstract pieces of metadata that are all that are available to you at the command line.

Yet as efficient as the graphical user interface (GUI) is at certain tasks, the command-line interface (CLI) has its advantages, too. Beyond just the capability to access it easily and without heavy graphical terminal clients, a host of functions exist that can be easily addressed only with textual commands. Sure, you can pick out five files in a folder of a hundred and select them visually with the mouse, if you know from their icons' appearance or placement that those are the files you need; but what if you wanted to delete all the files in a folder whose names begin with `temp` and end with `.jpg`? That's a task that involves some tricky gymnastics in the GUI—lots of clicking, some re-sorting of the file list, and careful visual coordination of your mouse with the files you want. But in the CLI, it's a single compact command: `rm temp*.jpg`.

This is just one example of an area where the Darwin CLI offers advantages over the Aqua GUI. There are a great many more, as you'll discover. You can monitor your system's disk usage and processing efficiency using almost instantaneous commands in the CLI, whereas in the GUI it requires you to open up information panels or even run applications that take several seconds at best to launch. What if your system suddenly slows to a crawl, the disk grinding away, and you want to know what's sucking up all the power? One possibility would be to navigate to the Activity Monitor application in the Utilities folder, double-click it, wait for it to launch, and then painfully click tabs and column headers to try to find out what's going on, while Activity Viewer itself fights for the system's resources to run. Or if you

have a Terminal window open, you can simply type **top
-ocpu** to pop up a textual representation of the very
same data that Activity Viewer gives you, only without
the overhead involved in launching a full-scale Aqua
application, giving you the information you need to
know immediately instead of making you wait.

The command line becomes even more important if
you intend to use Mac OS X in a server environment,
hosting a website or running a mail exchange agent or
a database. In this kind of situation, the Aqua GUI not
only doesn't help you much (especially after the server
software is set up and running properly), it can be
actively detrimental to the system's performance and
efficiency. You can't easily turn off Aqua the way you
can opt not to run KDE in Linux; but you can log in
remotely to the Darwin CLI shell, just as you would
on a Linux system, and modify the server's configuration files and perform maintenance as you need to
without having to swim through the pretty—but
unhelpful—Aqua GUI to get there. Even in the
best of circumstances, Aqua can be a boon to functionality if you're sitting next to the computer, but not
helpful for much else. The server might be locked
in a cabinet in a server room hundreds of miles away
from you; what good will candy-colored buttons
and translucent menus do you then? But a textual
command-line interface is just what the doctor
ordered.

Navigating the Filesystem

As in any Unix, the way files are organized is in a single large hierarchy of directories (folders) all leading up
to a single master directory, known as the *root* and

indicated with the slash (/) symbol. Disks (or, more
appropriately, their partitions or *volumes*) are attached at
various places in the hierarchy (*mount points*), wherever
their space is needed; in Mac OS X, these disks are
attached within the /Volumes directory. You can move
up and down the directory tree using the cd command,
as you'll see in Chapter 4, "Basic Unix Commands,"
going all the way up the hierarchy to the root level
and all the way down to a file that might be many
folders deep within a particular disk, such as /Volumes/
Macintosh HD/Users/btiemann/Documents/Taxes/2006/
Federal/Return.pdf. All files in the system are thus part
of the same filesystem hierarchy.

However, a graphical operating system like Mac OS
X—or, for that matter, like the classic Mac OS or
Windows—can't easily present its filesystem that way.
The root level, which contains many subdirectories full
of configuration files and system-level libraries, is not
just useless to the user—it's dangerous for the user to
have easy access to it. Suppose you opened up the icon
that represented your filesystem hierarchy, and you
were presented with a list of folders with names like
"Library", "bin", "etc", and "private". Imagine someone lacking in technical Unix expertise but brimming
with good intentions deciding to "clean up" his system
by throwing away some of these useless-looking folders. That would quickly spell disaster. And even if those
directories were hidden and well protected from acci-
dental deletion (as they are in Mac OS X, incidental-
ly), what kind of user interface would it be that made
you navigate down into the Volumes folder to find
your hard drives, your CDs and DVDs, and your other
disks and network resources? That's why Mac OS X,
like most graphical operating systems before it, chooses

instead to make the individual disks the topmost items
in navigation, each with its own hierarchy of files and
folders inside it.

The hard disk icons appear on your desktop and in
several places in the Finder, the navigation environment within the Mac OS X GUI. You select a disk by
its name and icon (much as you would select the C: or
A: drive in Windows) and begin to drill down into it,
starting at its top level where useful items are immediately accessible, with no need to navigate down into
any unfamiliar folder structures (see Figure 1.1).

Figure 1.1   Navigating into a disk in the
Mac OS X GUI.

In the Darwin CLI, though, navigation is another
matter. You have to always keep track of where in
the overall system hierarchy you are, not just within
the disk you happen to be exploring. Addressing a
file requires you to type in the entire path all the way
from the root on down, including the disk name. One

of the most flexible things about the CLI is that you can perform an action on a file anywhere in the system, no matter what folder your shell session is viewing, just by typing the file's complete path. However, unless you really need that kind of flexibility (when moving data between completely disparate parts of the system, for example), the need to type the entire path to a file or directory can be a detriment to your daily work. This is the reason why both the GUI and the CLI are focused on another special location in the system's landscape: the Home folder.

Your Home Folder

When you open a Finder window (select **File, New Finder Window** within the Finder), the first thing you see is the contents of your Home folder. This folder's name is the same as the "short name" you chose when creating your first user account at the time you set up your Mac, which might be your first name, your first name and last initial, or (as in my case) your first initial and last name—or something completely different. This is the first clue you might get, as a casual Mac user, as to the mysteries of the Unix layer underneath Mac OS X. Why this weird code name? Why not your full name?

The reason, as it turns out, has to do with the way Unix has been architected and implemented for decades. The "short name," as Apple calls it, is the same as the username or login name in Linux or Unix—the short, all-lowercase name that identifies the files and processes that you own to the Unix process table, forms the first part of your email address, and labels the folder in which all your files live in the multiuser world that is Unix. The username, as we'll refer to it from now on, cannot contain any spaces or nonalphanumeric characters, largely because it frequently comes into play in a variety of command-line contexts—as a token you pass to a CLI command, a name you type at the login prompt, and the name of many files and folders throughout the system, including your incoming mail file (a common feature on many Linux and Unix systems) and your Home folder. Because Unix commands and their parameters (*arguments*) are separated by spaces on the command line, a name that contains spaces would wreck the usual command structure unless very carefully handled. In short, making each user adopt a short, contiguous, easily typed string of letters or numbers as the user's ineffable name made a great many things much, much easier for the first versions of Unix to deal with architecturally— and so Mac OS X inherited that behavior and adheres to it in the name of cross-platform compatibility.

Traditionally, each user in a Unix system lives in a Home directory within the /home or /usr/home directory tree. The exact path varies from system to system; indeed on Windows, the same kind of structure exists, with arguably the strangest directory name of all: /Documents and Settings. In Mac OS X, the path to the user's Home folder is pretty simple: /Users. Thus, if my username is btiemann, my home folder name is /Users/btiemann.

NOTE: One way in which Mac OS X breaks with Unix tradition is in having capitalized names for its main structural folders: Applications, Library, System, Users. Traditionally, Unix systems would keep applications in /usr/bin or /usr/local/bin, libraries in

/usr/lib, system components in /usr/sbin or /sbin, and users' home folders in /usr/home or /home. The variety of alternative paths, and their names' relative meaninglessness at a casual observer's first glance, should give a pretty good explanation why Apple decided to try to bring some order to the chaos, at least for user-visible components such as Aqua apps. Nonetheless, compatibility with other Unix flavors forced Apple to maintain symbolic links to appropriate parts of the system with names like /etc and /var, mostly pointing to resources in the hidden /private directory.

For the sake of comparison, you can refer to the Filesystem Hierarchy Standard, a proposed (and often ignored) attempt at formalizing the architecture of Unix and its variants, at http://www.pathname.com/fhs/.

Coexisting with Other Users

Opening a Finder window or Terminal session starts you directly in your Home folder for a good reason: because that's where the files that concern you are stored. Theoretically, nothing outside your own Home folder can or should be changed, except in well-regulated procedures such as when you install software through a well-behaved script. Any documents, music files, videos, application preference files, or any other items created by you go into the appropriate folders within your Home folder. This makes it easy for you to back up your data—I just save what's in /Users/btiemann, and all my important stuff is preserved. But perhaps more significantly, it makes it possible for the Mac to be a fully multiuser computer, with each user encapsulated in an area that's under the user's control and nobody else's.

It might seem like overkill for the Mac, a desktop computer meant for technology novices and creative pros, to support the same kind of multiuser operation as the big-iron Unix systems used in the universities and research institutions where it was developed decades ago. After all, it's not like people need to time-share their cryptography research on your iMac, is it?

But think about this: A Mac in your house might be used not just by you, but by your spouse, kids, and guests as well, each of whom has the potential capability to mess up your data, delete your files, read your private information, or just cause inadvertent mischief such as moving your icons around enough so that your productivity is compromised. This, then, is the benefit of multiple users: Each person in your household can have his or her own user account, entirely separate from everyone else's, with its own music collection, its own desktop picture, its own loadout of Dock icons, and everything else personalized to each person's individual needs. Moreover, each person's data is kept private and hidden from every other user on the system. Data can be shared using the Shared folder (which everyone can put files into) or individual users' Public folders, so information that everyone needs access to can remain available and in sync. It's a little more effort to make every user log in individually to his or her own private session than to have everyone share one user account, but as long as you use the features built in to Mac OS X to make multiuser operation convenient—such as Fast User Switching, screen lockouts after an idle timeout, and a judicious password and administration policy—you'll find that it actually makes just as much sense to take advantage of the

Mac's multiuser nature in a home environment as it ever did in academia.

You should bear in mind, though, that because Mac OS X is designed to operate using the `sudo` model of privileged command execution, there is functionally no such thing as a directly usable "root" account; any command that operates on privileged processes or files (in other words, processes or files not owned by you) requires you to prove that you're an "admin user" by entering your password before the command is performed. This is accomplished using the `sudo` command, which precedes any privileged command-line string. For example, `ls ~otheruser/Desktop` will return a Permission Denied error; but **`sudo ls ~otheruser/ Desktop`** will prompt you for your own password, and then, if entered correctly, will execute the command. The `sudo` command will be discussed more thoroughly in Chapter 4, but as a general rule, if you try to issue a command that you find in this book (or that is based on what you find here) and you get a Permission Denied error, try preceding the command you're using with the `sudo` keyword to execute it with elevated privileges.

NOTE: Privileged actions are generally prevented outright in the GUI; for instance, you can't open another user's Desktop folder by double-clicking it, even if you're an admin user. Mac OS X doesn't give you the opportunity to "`sudo`" by entering your password, except in procedures such as software installation scripts. That you can use `sudo` to override permissions on the CLI is another example of its flexibility above and beyond what the GUI allows you to do, and a potential use for the CLI in a pinch.

Conclusion

Computing, by its nature, is a discipline that requires two levels of usability and flexibility: one for casual, day-to-day use and one for the more expert-level tweaking that happens at unexpected times. It's hard to imagine any single operating system that addresses both of those needs simultaneously and is all things to all people, while still remaining simple in execution and enjoyable to use. Few, however, would dispute that Mac OS X, in embodying two very different usage styles in a single unified operating system, is a big step in that direction, particularly compared to the specialized systems geared toward one audience or the other that have appeared in the past. As a demanding computer user, you'll come to appreciate not only the flexibility of the Unix underpinnings of Mac OS X, but also—when the time comes to put away the power tools and just enjoy using your computer—the simplicity and elegance of its graphical layer as well.

## 2

Configuring Your Terminal

You're probably already familiar with the basics of customizing your computer's desktop environment to suit your taste and work habits. Whether you're used to Mac OS X, Windows, or Linux, there are certain common interface tweaks—repositioning your taskbar or Dock, changing your desktop background, even swapping out your system's window decorations and fonts—that are designed not only to let you personalize your computer's aesthetics, but to mold it to your own personal style of computing. Like that groove in your sofa's cushions that you've spent years perfecting, your computer's interface is a reflection of you and won't quite fit anyone else.

This is why, when you venture into the Terminal application in Mac OS X, you'll want to make sure that you've made the appropriate customizations to it as well as to your Mac OS X system. Making the Unix command-line environment user friendly might seem like an oxymoron at first, but you'll find that after you've become accustomed to popping open a Terminal window to perform certain common tasks, having that Terminal window be personalized to your needs is a downright attractive idea. Indeed, a highly customized shell environment is what separates the true Unix geeks from the mere dabblers in the art.

Put Terminal in Your Dock

One of the first things you're going to want to do is make the Unix command line more accessible. Mac OS X doesn't go out of its way to make its Unix underbelly available for all users; because it's an operating system largely aimed at computer novices, this is hardly surprising. Apple's tech support staff likely dreads the phone call from someone's Aunt Peggy who accidentally clicked a couple of things and found herself confronted with a [My iMac:~] peggy% text prompt. Yet for the adventurous user, or the user who has a real interest in getting access to the dark side of the system, it's pointless to have to put up with the smoke and mirrors that Apple uses to distract us from it.

Terminal, the application you use to interface with the Unix command line, is found in the Utilities folder inside the Applications folder at the top level of your system hard disk. Open up a Finder window and navigate to it. (A shortcut is Shift+⌘+A, which takes you straight to the Applications folder.) Double-clicking the Terminal icon launches the application and puts you at the helm of the command line. Yet, to save yourself the effort of getting to this point in the future, you can put the Terminal application right into the Dock at the bottom of your screen; just drag the icon from the Finder window down into the Dock, anywhere on the left side of the dividing space. (The right side of the bar is for folders, documents, and mini-mized windows; the left side is for applications.)

From now on, the Terminal icon will live in the Dock, where you can rearrange its position with a simple drag to the left or right or remove it by dragging it off the Dock and dropping it anywhere else on the screen. (It's just a shortcut; removing the Terminal icon from the Dock doesn't delete the application from the system or anything.) But a single click on the icon in the Dock launches Terminal and opens a window, just as if you'd launched it from its location in the Utilities folder.

Set Dimensions, Colors, and Titles

Terminal → Preferences → Settings → Window

Launch the Terminal application with a single-click on its Dock icon or a double-click in a Finder window. The window that pops up is configured with the default color scheme and dimensions: black text on a white background, 80 columns wide, and 24 rows high. At the top, you see the greeting that will begin any command-line session from now on: `Welcome to Darwin!`

NOTE: Beginning with Mac OS X Leopard, Terminal supports a tabbed mode similar to how tabbed browsing works in Safari and other browsers. Rather than having multiple windows scattered around your screen, all your shell sessions—which, after all, are probably all the same size and shape—are contained within the same window and accessed by clicking their tabs below the title bar (you can turn it on and off by selecting **Show Tab Bar** from the **View** menu). You can choose to open new shell sessions in new windows or new tabs with the appropriate selections from the **Shell** menu.

In this book, just because it's more convenient, I'll refer to each shell session in Terminal as a *window*. Most configuration options apply equally in either mode.

The 80×24 window size is the default that's been handed down through the ages, from the versions of Unix that ran on PC hardware in text mode, where 80 columns by 24 rows was the de facto standard supported by all video cards at the time. Because of that fundamental limitation, most Unix programs are written to operate naturally in text screens no bigger than that basic 80×24 shape. Yet these programs will also usually take advantage of more columns or rows of text if they're available; because you're using what amounts to a virtual text screen within a much higher-resolution graphical display, you're free to make the Terminal window whatever size you like, even hundreds of columns wide and dozens of rows high—whatever your screen size will permit.

TIP: The green Zoom button, in the cluster of three round buttons in the top left of the window, is designed to resize the window of any application to its most efficient size—usually meaning the smallest it can be while still showing all the contents without scrollbars. In the case of Terminal, however, clicking the Zoom button maximizes the window to the full dimensions of your screen.

Resize the Terminal window the way you would any window: click and drag the bottom-right corner, and the dimensions are reflected in the title bar as you drag. You might find that your preferred Terminal screen size is more like 80 columns by 40 rows, or 132 columns by 30 rows. It's really up to you. But you don't have to be stuck manually changing the window size every time you open up a new Terminal window. You can set the default dimensions by choosing **Terminal, Preferences**, and then selecting the **Settings** section and the **Window** subsection. Enter the number of columns and rows to be used for newly opened windows, as well as the information to display in the title bar and the amount of data to hold in the scrollback buffer.

TIP: The Inspector palette, which in previous releases of Mac OS X was a much larger component of Terminal, now serves as a quick and direct way to set the window title and dimensions, as well as to view the names of any processes running in the frontmost shell window. Select **Shell, Show Inspector** to use it. In Leopard, the configuration options formerly available in the Inspector are now in the Settings section of the Terminal Preferences window.

The black-on-white color scheme might also not be quite to your liking. Many people find that a white background is hard on the eyes; or it might simply be more boring than you'd like. Fortunately, the Settings section of the Preferences window lets you customize your windows' color schemes to any of several prepackaged styles by choosing them from the list or by manually selecting the colors for the text, cursor, selected text, and highlighted (bold) text (in the **Text** subsection) or the background (in the **Window** sub-section). Clicking any of the color buttons brings up the standard Mac OS X color picker, which you can use to specify any color in the RGB spectrum, using any of several methods to indicate the one you want. Fiddle with the sliders until you get the color you're looking for.

You can customize any of the prepackaged color schemes, or you can create your own custom preset by clicking the + button at the bottom of the pane. After you've selected the right color scheme for your needs, click the Default button to set it as the scheme for all new windows.

TIP: Click the white "lozenge" button in the top-right of the title bar to display the choices of color palettes in a quick-selection bar. Double-clicking any item in this bar opens the Settings window for further customization.

NOTE: To set the transparency level of the window, select the color scheme to edit, then click Color and use the Opacity slider in the palette that appears.

Add Custom Key Mappings

Terminal → Preferences → Settings → Keyboard

Long-time Unix users will be interested in how Apple has integrated the Mac keyboard layout with the traditional Unix key commands that were primarily developed with PC-style keyboards. Mac keyboards have a number of keys that PC keyboards don't have, such as Help, Option, and Command (or Apple); they're also missing a few keys that Windows and Linux users have come to take for granted, such as Alt, Pause, and ScrollLock (which is used in systems such as Linux and

FreeBSD, even though it's hardly ever called for in Windows). To fully take advantage of the range of inputs supported by most Unix programs, Terminal supports key mappings to translate keystrokes on the Mac keyboard into key commands that Unix understands.

On the Mac, the various modifier keys all have specific meanings and functions. Command is meant to be combined, as a quick shortcut, with letter or number keys to execute commands that are normally found in menus. Option is used for performing "alternate" functions or creating "alternate" characters onscreen. Control, although hardly ever used in Mac OS X per se, is intended to help emulate the behavior of the Ctrl key found on PC keyboards. For example, the common Ctrl+C keystroke (usually written ^C), which cancels a command or process in Unix, would not be possible using the Mac's native modifier keys; Command+C means "copy," and Option+C creates a ç character. Thus, the Control key is there to help you perform the key commands you expect to be able to use in Unix, within the Terminal program or others that interact with foreign systems in the same way as if you were using a native keyboard. But some Unix key commands don't use the Ctrl key, and so you need to use another method if you're going to emulate them using the Mac's keyboard.

Terminal comes with most of the key commands you're likely to need already programmed in; these cover navigation keys such as Page Up/Page Down, Home, End, and some others (such as the Function keys, F1 and so on, at the top of the keyboard). You can add as many more combinations as you like, whether to emulate keystrokes that are possible only using a Windows keyboard or to simplify processes in commonly used Unix programs. To do so, or to view the existing key mappings, choose **Terminal, Preferences**, then go to the **Settings** section, then the **Keyboard** subsection.

Click **+** to set up a new key mapping. Choose a key to use in the mapping (only certain keys are available, but the F keys are good candidates for mapping to commonly used functions), select a modifier key to use in conjunction with it, and then specify what Terminal should do when the key combination is pressed. Most commonly, you will want to choose **send string to shell:** and then enter the string of characters that the combination should send.

NOTE: As you press keys to specify the string to send, notice that the control codes for each key are captured, rather than being interpreted as in an editing field; this includes the Delete key, which can't be used to backspace over mistakes here. Use the **Delete** button to erase incorrectly pressed keys.

There's no limit on the number of key combinations you can set up here. Through judicious allocation of your F keys and use of the available modifier keys, you can set up quick shortcuts even to your esoteric Emacs key bindings.

Change Your Shell

chsh

The default shell in Mac OS X is bash, the Bourne Again Shell. This command environment will be familiar to users of Linux, where it is the default shell as well. It's compatible with the original Bourne shell (sh), the accepted standard command interpreter for script programming, and it has many advanced features, such as command completion using the Tab key, command-line history recall and editing, and variable manipulation in scripts.

For most users' purposes, bash is more than adequate. However, you might be more familiar with another shell, such as tcsh (the standard shell in FreeBSD), ksh, or zsh. These shells are all bundled with Mac OS X, and you can switch your default shell to any of the following:

```
/bin/bash
/bin/csh
/bin/ksh
/bin/sh
/bin/tcsh
/bin/zsh
```

To change the shell that's executed when you launch a Terminal window, you can just set a new one in the Terminal Preferences; but for a more universal solution, one that ensures you get the desired shell even if you SSH in from a different machine, you need to change the shell down in the Unix level. To do this, enter **chsh**, which places you in the vi editor:

```
# Changing user database information for btiemann.
#
# (use "passwd" to change the password)
##
# Local NetInfo Database
##
Shell: /bin/bash
```

```
Full Name: Brian Tiemann
~
~
~
~
~
~
~
~
~
```

Use the arrow keys to move your cursor over the b in bash, and then press I to enter insert mode. Delete bash and replace it with, for example, **tcsh**. Then press Escape, enter :w and press Return to save the file, and then enter :q to quit.

From now on, any login session that you begin—whether through the Terminal or a remote SSH session—will use your newly specified shell.

NOTE: In the Terminal Preferences, make sure that **Execute the Default Login Shell Using /usr/bin/login** is the selected option; otherwise, it will not automatically execute the shell now specified in your user information in Unix.

Another, more graphical way to change your shell is to use the Advanced Options dialog in the Accounts pane in System Preferences. Right-click on a user and select Advanced Options to reveal this window. You can then choose a new shell from the drop-down menu, as well as changing other options (although you should only mess with them if you're sure you know what you're doing, because a misstep could cause the account to become unusable).

Execute a Command Upon Opening a Terminal Window or Tab

Terminal → Preferences

Changing your shell is great if you just want to switch to another command interpreter that you happen to prefer over the default bash. But standard shells are only one kind of program that can be launched to handle your login session. Instead of a shell, you might choose to run a MU* or IRC client, a text-driven net-worked information system, a news ticker—anything your needs dictate. Technically any Unix program can be invoked instead of a shell—even a command like ls; but typically you'd use a program that acts *like* a shell, by running continuously and interpreting input commands until it is explicitly quit by the user.

TIP: Type `telnet towel.blinkenlights.nl` to see a prime example of an alternative program used instead of a login shell: It's a real-time reenactment of the orig-inal *Star Wars*, rendered entirely in ASCII text art.

Terminal gives you the option to run any specified Unix program upon launching a new window, rather than your regular login shell. To do this, first open the Preferences window (accessible from the Terminal menu), then select the **Startup** section. Then, next to **Shells open with**, select the **command (complete path)** option, and replace whatever is in the text field with the command path to whatever program you want to run when you launch any Terminal window. (Note, however, that this only applies when you're running Terminal; your regular login shell is invoked if you SSH in from a remote computer.)

TIP: If you need to run certain commands at the beginning of a regular login shell session, such as declaring shell variables or expanding your command path, you can put those commands into your `.profile` file (or `.cshrc`, if you're using `tcsh`) to have them executed automatically while launching your command-line shell. See Chapter 6, "Viewing and Editing Text Files," for more about editing text files.

Save and Restore a `Terminal` Session

Terminal windows (and multi-window or multi-tab sets, known as *window groups*) can be saved—including their dimensions, colors, positions on the screen, and even a specific command to run—and restored at any time. This can be a great boon for someone who needs to maintain various websites and likes to keep each one's remote login session separate using a particular background color or window shape. First, configure your Terminal window (or windows or tabs) just the way you want them, using the Settings window (as described earlier in this chapter). Then choose **Window, Save Windows as Group.** In the dialog box that appears, specify a name for the session you want to save, and whether you want this window group to be treated as the default (so that all the saved windows are reopened whenever you launch Terminal).

TIP: Prior to Leopard, Terminal saved its sessions as `.term` files in `Library/Application Support/Terminal` within your Home folder. Now, though, each window group is an object stored as part of your preferences for Terminal, and kept in XML format in the com.apple.Terminal.plist file.

Later, you can restore any saved session by choosing **Window, Open Window Group** and then picking the saved window group you want. All your windows and tabs are restored to the condition they were in when they were saved.

View Your Command History

```
history
```

As you familiarize yourself with the Unix command-line environment, you'll find yourself typing more and more complex commands. Sooner or later will come a time when you're trying to re-create some command you'd issued only a few minutes before, but all the obscure little parameters and arguments escape your memory. Fortunately, modern shells (such as bash) take the guesswork out of this part of Unix by preserving your command history to be recalled for reference at any time.

The history command shows you all the commands you've issued during the current login session (which, by the way, are stored in the .bash_history file in your Home directory):

```
Silver:~ btiemann$ history
   1  ls
   2  exit
   3  exit
   4  ls
```

```
5  ls -a
6  ps -wwwaux
7  man launchctl
8  open .cshrc
9  history
```

Run a Previous Command Again

After you've printed out your command history and found out the ID number of a previously issued command that you want to run again, you can do so using a shortcut command sequence: the ! character, followed by the number of the command. For example, in the output of history, we found that the ps -wwwaux command is #6. We can reissue that command by entering !6.

```
Silver:~ btiemann$ !6
ps -wwwaux
```

Another shortcut is the !! sequence, which is shorthand for "run the previous command again":

```
Silver:~ btiemann$ !!
ps -wwwaux
```

Finally, for even more direct access to your command history, press the up- and down-arrow keys. This allows you to scroll through your previous commands one by one until you find the one you need; you can then move back and forth through the command string using the left- and right-arrow keys and edit the command to make any changes that are necessary before pressing Return to execute it.

Create a Command Alias

Another way to deal with the increasing complexity of Unix CLI commands as you become deeper immersed in the system is to create aliases to commonly used command strings, allowing you to enter only a two- or three-letter command to invoke a longer or more clumsy command.

In bash, you make an alias like this:

```
Silver:~ btiemann$ alias lr="ls -lrt"
```

This command assigns the shortcut lr to stand in for ls -lrt, a command that prints a file listing showing all items with full information, sorted by the date of last modification. This alias remains in place throughout the login session, until the window is closed.

You can also make aliases persistent, meaning that they're always available in every login shell, without you having to define them every time. To do this, you'll need to add the appropriate alias command into your .profile file, which is a startup script that is executed by bash every time you launch a new Terminal window.

You can't open the .profile file directly in an application like TextEdit, because in accordance with Unix tradition, any file whose name begins with a period is treated as "invisible" by the Mac OS X file picker.

However, from the command line, you can use the open command to launch the file into TextEdit.

```
Silver:~ btiemann$ open .profile
2007-01-17 01:10:25.449 open[6939] No such file:
  /Users/btiemann/.profile
```

Oops! Looks like the .profile file doesn't exist yet, and we can't create it using TextEdit—not without having to wrestle with nonstandard filename extensions and such. No matter: Use the touch command to create it:

```
Silver:~ btiemann$ touch .profile
Silver:~ btiemann$ open .profile
```

There. Now the file has been opened in TextEdit, and you can add the alias line to it:

```
alias lr="ls -lrt"
```

Save the file. Now, if you open a new Terminal window, you'll find that the lr command is built in, ready to be executed at any time.

TIP: My machine's name is Silver, and so my prompt looks like you see it here: Silver:~ btiemann$. It will reflect your machine's name as defined in the system's Sharing Preferences.

You can change the format of your prompt in the .profile file using any of a number of formatting codes, as described quite well here:

http://penguinpetes.com/b2evo/index.php?title=tweak in_your_bash_prompt

---

TIP: You can set default aliases (and other shell settings) for all users in the system by putting them into the global profile file, /etc/profile. This file is read before the individual user's .profile file.

Conclusion

This chapter covered a few of the basic techniques for making your command-line environment comfortable and familiar. If you're new to the Unix world, it's completely understandable that it's esoteric and primitive-looking at first glance; but customizing your Terminal windows and your command history are some of the easiest ways to gain the psychological upper hand right away over the system's seeming weirdnesses.

The chapters following this one will deal more directly with the actual Unix commands you'll be able to issue at the shell prompt. It will all, however, depend on your ability to move comfortably around in the Terminal application and at the command line. The basic customization techniques covered in this chapter only scratch the surface of what you can do to make your Unix shell environment truly your own; by the time you're an expert, you'll have customized your shell prompt to reflect your current working directory, added a directory search path encompassing several custom locations for your own executable programs, and configured the cron scheduler to make your Mac shout "π-time!" at 3:14 in the morning. But for now, we've covered enough ground to start talking about how the Terminal can help us interact with the files we already know about in the graphical side of Mac OS X—and those that we never would otherwise have seen.

## 3

Using the Command Line

If you're a casual Mac user, or even if you're a hard-core Linux or Unix user, there are a few things about Mac OS X and the particular flavor of Unix under its candylike shell that might catch you off guard. Files and folders behave in rather different ways when you're addressing them with textual commands than when you're shoving them around with your mouse. Not only do they look different, they act different, too. You might even say they "think different."

The shell, which is what we call the command-line environment displayed by the Terminal application, is an austere and cryptic piece of software—about as un-Mac-like as it can possibly get. By the end of this book, you'll have found all kinds of uses for it—tricks that weren't otherwise possible using the graphical Aqua interface. But there's a steep learning curve, particularly for readers who have never dabbled in Unix before, and there are a few things you're going to have to know about how your files work in the shell before you can really start ordering them around.

NOTE: This will be discussed in more detail in Chapter 4, "Basic Unix Commands," but you should be aware that every Unix command is fully documented within the command line using the man ("manual") command. Type **man** *command* to learn more about any command you've heard about.

Everything Is a File

Your Mac is designed primarily to show you your documents, folders, applications, and other items in neatly ordered windows, with pretty icons next to them to help you differentiate them based on their type. You can open Finder windows that show you each item's Kind in a column, distinguishing your Photoshop images from your Word documents and your folders and applications. Mac OS X even has "bundles," which are special folders full of executables and other items masquerading as single monolithic files in the Finder, which you'll learn more about in Chapter 5, "Using the Finder." At the graphical level, your Mac is full of all kinds of items that each get their own unique look and descriptive vocabulary.

Not much of that matters at the command-line level. Your shell doesn't see a folder differently from how it sees a Word document; they're both just "streams of bits with names" as far as it's concerned, and in its 1970s-era worldview that's all that matters. The only thing distinguishing a folder (or *directory*) from a file is that the bits in it describe links to other files that the operating system should interpret as part of that folder, rather than the binary or textual data stream that make up a file's contents—but to Unix that's trivia. If you use the 1s ("list") command in the shell to list the files in a folder, you'll just get a list of names—no icons, no turn-down arrows, no clues to help tell you that some of the things you're looking at are files and some are folders, applications, or what-have-you. (There are some options you can give to the `ls` command to make it smarter about how it lists the items, as you'll see later; but that's a courtesy that Unix only grudgingly grants.)

In the Unix world, everything's a file, including such oddities as running processes and network connections and attached devices, and you interact with them all in pretty much the same way, using the same commands for everything (with a few exceptions, like the `mkdir` command). I point this out to make you aware that if you see the command-line examples in this book refer to "files," it means "files, folders, and any other discrete pieces of data." If a command makes a distinction between regular data files and other kinds of items, I'll say so; but otherwise, you can generally expect that a command will work the same on one kind of item as on another, because it'll see "files" with as little discrimination as Unix does.

File Types and Extensions

The Unix side of Mac OS X might not care about what makes one kind of file different from another, but the graphical side certainly does. The "kind" of a file, which you can view by selecting it and then choosing **File**, **Get Info**, is what determines what kind of icon it has in the Finder and, more importantly, what application it opens in when you double-click it. This is pretty basic stuff, and it's familiar to anyone who's used a Windows PC or Mac anytime in the past 20 years.

What you might not be familiar with is just *how* Mac OS X identifies a file's kind. In the old, pre-OS X days, files on the Mac had an invisible four-letter "Type" code, along with another four-letter "Creator" code, the combination of which told the system what application the file belonged to and what other apps could open it if they advertised themselves as being able to open, for example, "JPEG" pictures or "MooV" movie files. Because these codes were invisible, nobody had to deal with them or even know they were there, and—even better—nobody had to put up with those ugly "extensions" they'd seen on files in Windows or MS-DOS. Why should you have to name a file "Shopping List.txt" when you could just call it "Shopping List" and have the system *know* it was a text file because of its TEXT Type code?

Mac OS X brought an end to that happy and elegant time, to many users' (and my) chagrin. Now, instead of Type and Creator codes, files were identified using extensions, just like in Windows: .txt for text files, .doc for Microsoft Word documents, .jpg for JPEG pictures, and so on. On the face of it, this looks like a huge step backward for usability. But what it really was was a nod to reality; the world in 2001 was dominated by Windows, and that meant that every file on the Internet had extensions, so we might as well get used to it. But Mac users don't have to like it. And that's why extensions in Mac OS X, after some early rough edges were sanded off, are handled with arguably even more slickness and flexibility than Type and Creator codes were.

You can hide the extension on a file, on a per-file basis (unlike in Windows, where either all extensions are shown or only the unknown ones are, as dictated by a global setting). Better yet, the way you hide an extension is by simply renaming the file: You click the filename, you put the cursor at the end, you backspace out the .txt or .doc, and it's gone, just as if the extension were any meaningless and disposable part of the filename. But it's not really gone: Do a Get Info on the file, and you'll find that the .txt or .doc is still there—the Name & Extension field shows the complete name, and the Hide Extension check box is checked. The system is similarly smart enough to figure out whether to hide or show the extension when you save a new file in TextEdit or Preview; if you specify the extension, it's shown, but if you don't, it's hidden.

Why is this useful? Why not just use Type codes like in the old days? Well, think about interoperability. If the filenames didn't have extensions, and you sent a text file or an MP3 song to someone using Windows, his computer wouldn't know what to do with it. Windows and Linux can't read Type and Creator codes, and those codes aren't included with files when transferred through popular Internet apps anyway. But if the extensions are there, and they're hidden only for the benefit of Mac users, then Windows and Linux users can still open the files using their favorite text editors or MP3 players, and Mac users can still look at pretty, extensionless filenames. Everybody wins!

TIP: Rather than the "Creator" of each individual file being stored in metadata, Mac OS X keeps a database of "opener apps" for known file types. The default opener for JPEG images, for example, is Preview. You can set individual files to open in other apps, though, and you can change the default opener of a given file type; in the **Get Info** window, open up the **Open with** panel to configure these behaviors.

Be aware that just because you don't see an extension on a filename in the Finder, that doesn't mean the extension isn't there. If you look at the file in the command-line shell, you'll see the whole filename, extension and all.

TIP: Unix has its own, entirely separate way of figuring out what kind of files you're looking at: It looks at the file's contents and makes an educated guess. This functionality isn't part of your shell or any universal system service, though—it's accomplished using the file command, which you can use like so:

```
Silver:~/Pictures btiemann$ file pvp.psd
pvp.psd: Adobe Photoshop Image
```

Maximum Filename Lengths

One of the benefits that Mac OS X brought to the Mac-using world was longer filenames. In the old Mac OS, 31 characters were all you had to work with; you didn't have to worry about extensions, but 31 was still too short, for instance, for naming an MP3 file according to its title, artist, and album. MS-DOS, if your memory is that long, was even worse: eight characters, all in caps, and a three-letter extension. How did we ever survive?

But now we have a full 255 characters to devote to any filename, and that includes spaces, quotes, apostrophes, and all kinds of other characters (with a few exceptions, as you'll see shortly). I don't care how long the title of your favorite MP3 is; you're not going to run out of letters to describe it in Mac OS X.

One thing to watch out for, though, is that when filenames get too long to be displayed comfortably, they start to wreak havoc on the mechanisms used to display them, both in the graphical and command-line levels. The Finder will shorten a displayed filename to a reasonable length and stick an ellipsis (…) in the middle to show you that there's more to the filename than what you see. But the Unix shell is less sophisticated and will dutifully print out the whole massive filename, even if it wraps four times in your 80-column-wide display and wrecks the format of your file listing. To keep your own sanity, to say nothing of good desktop hygiene, you should probably keep your filenames to around 30–40 characters at most. But that's just some motherly advice, not a requirement of the system.

Case Sensitivity and Case Preservation in Filenames

Where Mac OS X differs most visibly from other Unixes is in the way its filesystem (HFS+, for those of you keeping score) handles capitalization in filenames. Most Unix-style operating systems are *case sensitive*, meaning that a file called `File1.txt` is entirely distinct from one called `file1.txt`, and both can happily exist in the same folder. Linux or FreeBSD will see not the slightest similarity between those two files, no matter how much our human sensibilities might tell us that they're the same.

Mac OS X, like the classic Mac OS before it, is *not* case sensitive; it doesn't care whether you said `File1.txt` or `file1.txt`. Only one of them can exist in a folder at the same time, and there's no ambiguity for either computers or humans in telling which file you meant. Even Unix commands like `ls` will work if you give them filenames to operate on that don't match the capitalization of the actual files (try it: `ls /library`).

NOTE: Because bash and other shells packaged with Mac OS X were developed outside Apple and without this kind of flexible case handling in mind, Tab completion won't work unless you use the correct capitalization. For instance, typing **/lib** and pressing Tab won't do anything, but **/Lib** followed by Tab will expand to **/Library**.

However, unlike some versions of Windows, Mac OS X is also *case preserving*. If you create a file called `file1.txt`, the system will keep it as `file1.txt`; it won't helpfully capitalize the first letter for you, it won't force the whole thing to uppercase or lowercase, and it won't lose track of the capitalization if you send the file through one application and then another, or up to a web server and back down again. Things stay the way you put them, but the system can generally figure out what you mean if you're less precise than it is. Unix purists who insist that the byte for "a" is as different from "A" as it is from "9" might grouse, but Mac OS X is just behaving the way humans do, isn't it?

Nonetheless, there's something weird about how Mac OS X's Unix shell lists files: it distinguishes between uppercase and lowercase letters when alphabetizing, and uppercase words come first in the ASCII code page. Thus, a file listing at the command line will be sorted differently from one in the Finder, with all the items whose names begin with capital letters listed before the ones in lowercase.

NOTE: Mac OS X's case-handling behavior is a feature of the HFS+ (Mac OS Extended) filesystem, Apple's standard disk format. Other filesystem types, such as UFS and ZFS, are available for experts; because they're pure Unix filesystems, their case handling is in the Unix vein: case sensitive and case preserving.

Special Characters to Avoid in Filenames

Every operating system has some restrictions it places on what characters you can use in filenames, and Mac OS X is no exception. In fact, it actually has more complexity to worry about than most systems, if you're going to be working with the shell as much as with the Finder.

Like other Unixes, the command-line portion of Mac OS X forbids you from using the forward-slash (/) character in filenames. This is because slashes are used to delimit directory names in paths; for example, /Users/btiemann/Documents/File1.txt represents a file four folders down from the system root. I can't name a file Taxes/2006.pdf, because the system would think I'm talking about a subfolder called Taxes with a file called 2006.pdf inside it.

Okay, so slashes are fairly easy to avoid. But if you're checking my work, you'll have noticed that you can create a "Taxes/2006.pdf" file without any trouble in the Finder. What gives?

The answer is that, historically, the classic (pre-OS X) Mac OS allowed slashes—because it used the colon (:) as its path delimiter, not the slash. When Mac OS X came out, rather than forcing everyone to go through an upgrade procedure to rename all their files with slashes in the names, it simply interpreted those files on the command line with colons instead of slashes. Similarly, if you create a file at the command line with a colon in it, it will show up as a slash in the Finder. Try it: type **touch blah:foo** at the command line, and watch the file "blah/foo" appear in the corresponding Finder window.

The upshot is that you can't use colons in the Finder, and you can't use slashes in the shell—but the reverse in both cases is perfectly legal. If you have trouble keeping this straight, don't worry: you're not alone. (Or should that be "don't worry/you're not alone"?)

That's not where the inconveniences end, unfortunately. There's also the unpleasant matter of spaces, apostrophes, quotes, dashes, asterisks, and other characters that seem perfectly natural as names of documents but that will cause you fits if you try to work with them on the command line. Each of the character classes in Table 3.1 has a special meaning for Unix, one that doesn't normally impinge on your life in the Finder, but that can make the shell fall over and twitch if you don't know what you're doing.

Table 3.1   **Avoiding Special Characters in Filenames**

Character	Meaning
Space	Separator between command arguments
/	Path delimiter
\	Escapes the following character
-	Can indicate a command option
[]	Shell scripting tokens
{}	Shell scripting tokens
*	Wildcard (multiple characters)
?	Wildcard (single character)
'	Command argument grouping delimiter
"	Command argument grouping delimiter

To use any of the preceding characters in a filename in the shell, you have to *escape* it—precede it with a backslash character, which tells the shell to treat the next character in the filename literally, not as a special command character. For instance, suppose you have a file called My "Road Trip" CDs.txt that you want to address using a shell command (ls). You'd have to write the command like this:

```
Silver:~ btiemann$ ls My\ \"Road\ Trip\"\ CDs.txt
```

This tells the shell that the spaces and quotes are part of the filename, not separate arguments for the ls command. Otherwise, ls would be trying to list three separate files: one called My, another called Road Trip, and a third called CDs.txt.

TIP: The command-line completion feature of the bash shell can mitigate most of the pain associated with special characters in filenames. For example, type ls

My and then press Tab, and unless other files in the folder have names that start with My, bash will automatically fill out the rest of the file with all the special characters escaped for you. This helps only when you're addressing existing files, though; you still have to do all the escaping yourself if you're creating a new file or applying a new name.

To keep your command-line life simple, I'd recommend that you just avoid using weird characters like the ones described here. For files that you plan on using only in the GUI side of Mac OS X, it's okay to use whatever letters the Finder will accept. But your life on the command line will be a lot happier if you leave out the spaces, quotes, and asterisks in the files you create there.

Wildcards and What They Mean

Wait. What? Wildcards? What's that about?

Unless your computing career has encompassed Unix/Linux or MS-DOS, wildcards will be something new to you. They're unique to command-line operating system environments and are also a key part of their usability. Wildcards are what allow you to specify groups of files all at once, based on similarities in their filenames.

The asterisk (*) character can be used to represent any contiguous series of characters, and the question mark (?) can represent any single character. Using these wildcard characters, you can perform repetitive or tedious tasks on large groups of files all at once, instead of having to do it over and over, once per file. For instance, consider the following list of files:

```
Picture01.jpg
Picture02.jpg
Picture03.jpg
Pics.txt
```

Suppose you wanted to get a list of only the JPEG files in this directory. That could be accomplished in any of several ways:

```
Silver:~ btiemann$ ls *.jpg
Silver:~ btiemann$ ls Picture0?.jpg
Silver:~ btiemann$ ls Pict*
```

As you can see, wildcards in Unix don't discriminate between the filename and the extension; the asterisk wildcard covers the .jpg part of the affected files as well as the unspecified portion before the period. This differs from the MS-DOS way, in which you had to specify *.* to refer to all the files in a directory. In Mac OS X and other Unixes, you can use * to cover everything.

Another kind of wildcard that gives you more precise control is the brackets ([]), which lets you specify a set of matching characters (instead of the "any character" that the ? wildcard implies). Any characters specified within the brackets are potential matches. For example:

```
Silver:~ btiemann$ ls Picture0[13].jpg
Picture01.jpg          Picture03.jpg
```

NOTE: Wildcards don't work on "hidden" files, which you'll learn more about in Chapter 4, "Basic Unix Commands." In other words, a "hidden" file (a file whose name begins with a period, such as .login) will not appear in a listing generated by ls *, nor will it be deleted by rm *. You have to delete hidden files manually, one by one.

You might be accustomed to selecting large groups of files in a Finder window, visually, to move or delete them all in one fell swoop. This might seem a more direct solution than wildcards, and in many cases it is. But if the files are all named similarly enough that they can all be described using a wildcard or two, and if the Finder can't group them efficiently, you might find that using the Terminal and wildcards can save you some time over doing it the Finder's way.

Conclusion

If this book is your first introduction to Unix, you'll be tackling it with less first-hand guidance than I had when I was first shown a SunOS login shell in 1994. It's a rare and adventurous soul who dives straight into the world of the Unix shell and tries to learn all about it on his own, without a mentor or guru handy to point out the pitfalls and offer helpful shortcuts. There are so many of these potential traps that even a thick book dedicated to Unix can't cover them all; only experience can give you the familiarity you need to be completely fluent and efficient at the shell. Still, this chapter attempts to provide the cornerstones to an understanding of what kinds of expectations Unix has of you, the user; and in the process, you will have learned how to extrapolate from what you know to find out how to overcome the rest of the obstacles you'll encounter.

## 4

Basic Unix Commands

This chapter discusses the fundamental commands that you use in everyday computing at the Unix shell—the commands that give you the mobility and visibility in plain text that you're used to in the rich graphics of the Finder and the Aqua layer. These are the commands that let you list files, move from folder to folder, examine files' characteristics, create folders, move and copy files around, and—perhaps most important—find out more about what these commands can do if you give them the right options.

Unix might seem impenetrable at first, defying your accustomed mouse-and-menu computing skills; but with these basic commands at your disposal, it'll soon turn into a degree of freedom that you'll wonder how you ever did without.

List Items in a Folder

```
ls
```

If there's such a thing as *the* most basic Unix command, it's ls, which stands for "list." It's the functional equivalent of opening up a Finder window to see the files and folders in it. In its simplest form, entering the ls command gives you a simple list of the names of the items in your current working directory (which, when you first open a Terminal window, is your Home folder):

```
Silver:~ btiemann$ ls
Desktop            Movies            Public
Documents          Music             Sites
Library            Pictures
```

Like the Finder, though, ls has a great many options that let you customize how your files are displayed. Just as the Finder can be customized to show you your files' sizes, last-modified dates, and types, or to list them alphabetically, by size, and so on, the ls command has options to suit your every need, as you'll soon see.

TIP: It's easy to see what your current folder is in the Finder—its name is printed at the top of each window. In the Unix shell, it's a little more tricky. Your prompt is what shows you your current directory's path, but you have to do a little decoding.

```
Silver:~/Documents/Taxes btiemann$
```

The btiemann part isn't part of the path, though it might look like it. What it indicates is your Unix username. The path is on the left side of the prompt, following the machine name and the colon. In Unix, the tilde (~) character is shorthand for "my Home directory," which in my case is /Users/btiemann. (You can use any other user's username to go to that user's Home directory, too.) So the path ~/Documents/Taxes is really /Users/btiemann/Documents/Taxes, although you can use the tilde to represent your Home directory in any command and thus save yourself some typing.

The most common *argument* (parameter) for ls, though, is the name of a folder to list instead of the one you're currently in:

```
Silver:~ btiemann$ ls Documents
Letters          Taxes          shopping list.txt
```

This is a *relative* path, where you specify the name of a folder directly inside the one you're in. If you want to list a folder somewhere else in the system, you'll need to specify an *absolute* path, beginning with the slash (or the ~, which signifies your Home directory):

```
Silver:~ btiemann$ ls /Library
Silver:~ btiemann$ ls ~/Pictures/Alaska
```

NOTE: Another way to address items outside your present directory is to use the .. construct, which means "this directory's immediate parent directory." This technique, which can be used to form relative paths to items anywhere in the system, is discussed later in this chapter.

List Items with Sizes and Type Symbols

```
ls -skF
```

Now it's time to try some command-line options (also known as flags). Options usually take the form of a dash (-) and a single letter, although longer strings are also often used, depending on the command. Options are generally specified before the files or folders the command pertains to.

The first option to demonstrate is -s, which causes ls
to print a size next to each file's name and a total size
for the folder's contents at the top:

```
Silver:~ btiemann$ ls -s Pictures
total 17960
    0 Alaska              82 Yosemite.jpg
```

A little investigation will show you that these size
numbers are twice what they should be. That's because
by default your shell shows file sizes as the number
of 512-byte blocks on the disk they occupy, not the
number of kilobytes. To express sizes in kilobytes,
combine the -s option with -k to form -sk:

```
Silver:~ btiemann$ ls -sk Pictures
total 8980
    0 Alaska              41 Yosemite.jpg
```

TIP: If you don't want to have to use the -k option
every time, you can set your default block size to 1K by
adding the following two lines to your .profile file:

```
BLOCKSIZE=K
export BLOCKSIZE
```

This is such a handy and essential step that I'm going
to do all the upcoming examples with my block size set
to 1K, just to simplify everything.

That's better. But what about that pesky Alaska entry?
It's not an empty file with zero contents; it's a folder. If
this were the Finder, this would be obvious because of
its familiar folder icon. But on the command line, we
have to use another option to append special identify-
ing characters to filenames based on their types: -F.

```
Silver:~ btiemann$ ls -skF Pictures
total 8980
   0 Alaska/             41 Yosemite.jpg
```

Aha! Alaska now has a trailing slash, which means it's a folder. Other kinds of files that are distinguished by trailing symbols are executables (*), symbolic links (@), sockets (=), whiteouts (%), and FIFOs (|). Don't worry about knowing what the last few are; you're not likely to run into them.

TIP: Have a bunch of very large files whose sizes you want to see expressed in megabytes or gigabytes? See "Express File Sizes in Terms of Kilo/Mega/Gigabytes" later in this chapter.

List Items with Color-Coded Types

`ls -G`

Don't get your hopes up: Unix can't distinguish among different kinds of data files the way the Finder can. You won't be able to tell your image files apart from your Word documents by trailing icon characters, or anything like that. All you get are their names. (This is, oddly enough, an area where filename extensions—ugly though they might be—come in handy.)

You can, however, supplement or supplant your `ls -F` output with color coding. If you use the -G option, the different kinds of files that are distinguished by trailing symbols with the -F option are printed in different colors: blue for folders, red for executables, purple for symbolic links, and a few additional color styles, such as black on a green background for directories that are writable by other users (see Chapter 7, "Ownership and Permissions," for more about how files and folders are protected against unauthorized access).

```
Silver:~ btiemann$ ls -G
Desktop              Movies              Public
Documents            Music               Sites
Library              Pictures
```

You can't tell in print, but trust me: These folder names are all printed in blue now.

TIP: If you want to build certain options into every ls command you run, you can do so by creating an alias, also called ls, which overrides the plain ls command with a compound command such as ls -skFG. See Chapter 2, "Configuring Your Terminal," for more on creating aliases.

List Specific Items Matching a Pattern (Using Wildcards)

```
ls *.png
```

Wildcards are useful filtering mechanisms, allowing you to list only the files whose names match a certain pattern, as well as to apply any other command to only those filtered files.

Recall that the * wildcard matches any string of characters, and the ? wildcard matches any single character. Thus, you can list only the PNG files in your Pictures folder like this:

```
Silver:~ btiemann$ ls Pictures/*.png
Banzai.png          Half Dome.png      Yosemite3.png
```

Or you can match all Excel spreadsheets and templates like this:

```
Silver:~ btiemann$ ls Documents/*.xl?
Vacation Expenses.xls    Expenses.xlt
```

View Hidden Files and Folders

```
ls -A
```

As you might already know, the Finder doesn't show you all the files that are in a given folder; sometimes it hides items from you that you generally don't need to see, such as the Unix directories at the root level (like /etc, /var, and the like). Although the Unix shell enables you to view many of these items directly, there are still some kinds of files that are hidden even in the shell. These are typically files that you yourself choose to make invisible so they don't clutter up your file listing; they're usually configuration files for your shell or other Unix programs you might use. The conventional method for hiding a file is to put a period (.) at the beginning of its name. Thus, files and directories like .profile, .forward, and .ssh are all hidden if you do a plain ls command.

Yet sometimes you'll want to see all these files so you can get an accurate census of what's in your home folder. To do this, use the -A option:

```
Silver:~ btiemann$ ls -A
.DS_Store        Desktop         Music
.MacOSX          Documents       Pictures
.Trash           Library         Public
.profile         Movies          Sites
```

If you use the -a option instead, the directory entries .
and .. (the current and parent directories, respectively)
are also listed.

TIP: Normally the Finder hides the "dotfiles" the same
way the Unix shell does. You can override this behavior
and make the Finder do the equivalent of ls –A by
issuing the command:

```
Silver:~ btiemann$ defaults write com.apple.
Finder AppleShowAllFiles yes
```

List Permissions, Ownership,
and Other Details

```
ls -l
```

There's a lot more to your files than just their names,
vague sizes, and types. You'll also want to know their
last-modified dates, Unix permissions, and the exact
number of bytes each one consists of. This is where
the -l (for "long") option comes into play.

```
Silver:~ btiemann$ ls -l
total 0
drwx------    17 bct bct   578 Jan 25 21:54 Desktop
drwx------    81 bct bct  2754 Jan 24 09:03 Documents
drwx------    54 bct bct  1836 Dec 11 08:11 Library
drwx------   196 bct bct  6664 Oct 29 22:44 Movies
drwx------    66 bct bct  2244 Sep 22  2005 Music
drwx------   179 bct bct  6086 Dec 31 10:50 Pictures
drwxr-xr-x     6 bct bct   204 Apr 21  2005 Public
drwxr-xr-x   303 bct bct 10302 Oct 10  2005 Sites
```

Whew—there's a lot of stuff here. It's starting to look more like the Finder's List view, rather than the listings we've seen so far, which have more in common with Icon view. The columns of information aren't the same as what the Finder presents, though; in fact, with the names of the files on the far right, it almost looks like a mirror-image version of List view. With the exception of the Size and Date Modified columns, the two views show quite different sets of information. Let's start at the right and move left through the columns.

Second from the right is the date of each item's last modification. If the file was last changed less than a year ago, the time of day is also shown; otherwise, it shows the year.

Next to that is the size of the file in bytes. This is a straightforward measurement for files; but for folders, it represents the size of the index data contained in the folder, which points to all the files inside it. It's a number that increases as you add more files to the folder, but otherwise it's not a directly useful number.

Next, moving left, is the name of the group that owns the file. To the left of that is the user who owns it. As you'll see in Chapter 7, each item has both a user owner and a group owner, which allows you to specify who should have access to the file for reading and modifying it—a user that's part of a special group might be given write access, but other users can only read it, for example. In the case of these files, just to make things confusing, the group that owns the file has the same name as my user account because it's my own personal group, created at the same time as my user account. This will all make more sense later on.

NOTE: The format of this book makes it impossible to show the file listing using my full username (bctiemann), so I've changed it to "bct" in this example file listing just to illustrate what goes where. The files in your home directory will be owned by the same Unix username as is used for the name of your Home directory.

Next is a column showing the number of items in each listed folder, or—if the item is a file—the number of hard links to it. Hard links are a fairly esoteric concept that you'll learn more about in Chapter 5, "Using the Finder."

Finally, at the far left, we get to the permissions string. This is where things get really interesting. Chapter 7 discusses the mechanics of file access permissions in detail, but right here you don't need to know how to manipulate such things—just how to interpret them.

Permissions are expressed in a string of 10 characters, such as `drwxr-xr-x`. Each one of these characters represents a certain kind of permission right. Ignore the first character (`d` here) for now; the important ones are the remaining nine, which you can think of as being three groups of three. Each of these groups represents a type of user who might be accessing the file: in order, the file's user owner, the file's group owner, and everybody else. Within each of the three groups are three types of permission: read, write, and execute. Thus, putting all this together, you can read the third character (`w`) as being "write permissions for the file's user owner" and the eighth (`r`) as being "read permissions for everybody."

TIP: Using vertical bars to divide the conceptual groups in the permissions string, you can read it like this: d|rwx|r-x|r-x

---

The purpose of permissions is to grant or deny access to certain kinds of users, and the permissions string indicates who is allowed and denied to do what. A letter (r, w, or x) is shown in a certain position only if the corresponding permission is granted. If it's not, a dash (-) is shown. Thus, the sixth permission character (-) in this string example means that write permissions are *not* granted to users in the owner group. But those users *are* allowed to read and execute the file because the r and x characters (*bits*) are there in their corresponding positions.

User permissions override group permissions, which also override other permissions; so if you're in the owner group (which doesn't have write permission) *and* you're the file's owner (who *does* have write permission), you do get to modify the file.

Most regular files in your Home folder have the permissions string -rw-r--r--, which means that anybody can read it, but only you can write or modify it. (If the file is owned by someone else, then only that person can modify it; you can't.) There are some other kinds of permissions strings you'll encounter, though, such as the one you saw before, drwxr-xr-x. This is the typical permissions string for a folder (or directory), which is what the d in the first position means. The "write" bit, when found on a directory, refers to the ability to put new files into it, or to rename or delete files in it (if *those* files' permissions permit it). The "execute" bit usually makes it possible to type a program file's name and execute it as a command; but when the item is a directory, what the x means is that users can list its contents and the contents of its subdirectories (the r bit is not enough for this).

Many more kinds of permissions appear on files throughout Mac OS X. The first character can be l, b, s, or any of several other symbols that represent special kinds of files, such as symbolic links, block devices, and named sockets. There are also the setuid and setgid modes, which allow an executed program to attain the access credentials of another user, which isn't normally possible. When these modes are active, the x and - symbols are replaced by s and S. You most likely won't have to worry about these arcane details, though; if you focus on being able to read permissions strings like -rw-r--r-- (a file that anyone can read and the owner can edit) and drwx------ (a directory that only the owner can read), then you'll understand the vast majority of what's important in Unix permissions.

You can, of course, change the ownership and permissions on files; but that's a topic unto itself, and covered in detail in Chapter 7, "Ownership and Permissions."

NOTE: Because the full file listing you get with ls -l is a bit too wide to print comfortably in a book this size, I'll be removing the user and group ownership columns from file listings in the rest of this chapter, unless they're significant to what's being demonstrated.

Sort Contents by Date and Time

```
ls -lt
ls -ltr
```

File listings aren't much use without the capability to sort them and quickly find the items you're looking for, whether by name or by other criteria such as the time they were last modified. In the Finder, you'd select a column to sort on by clicking the column header and then clicking it again to reverse the order of the listing. In the shell, though, such viewing options are controlled by command-line options, like -t, which sorts by the last-modified time. When combined with the -l option, you get a detailed and sorted listing, just like in the Finder's List view.

When specifying multiple options for ls, it's possible to type them all out individually, such as ls -l -t. But that's not necessary; as a shortcut, you can combine them into a single argument: ls -lt.

```
Silver:~ btiemann$ ls -lt Desktop/
total 44812
-rw-r--r--  8012565 Jan 21 16:01 Skydive.mp4
-rw-r--r--  3191015 Jan 14 16:36 Red Rain.mp3
-rw-r--r--   139838 Jan 13 18:50 dogcookie.jpg
-rw-r--r--      382 Jan  3 20:19 Stocks.rtf
-rw-r--r--      365 Dec 11 12:35 draperies.rtf
-rw-r--r--    10682 Dec  6 14:40 comics.rtf
```

As you can see, the contents are sorted by date and time now, not by name. To reverse the listing (which is useful if you've got a long file listing and you want to find the most recently changed items by putting them at the bottom), combine the command with the -r option:

```
Silver:~ btiemann$ ls -ltr Desktop/
```

NOTE: Technically, you can issue these commands without the -l option, and the files will still be sorted according to the last-modified time or by whatever other criteria you specify—just not in the detailed columnar listing. I'm giving the examples with the -l component, though, because that's how you'll be doing these kinds of listings the majority of the time.

Sort Contents by Size

`ls -lS`

Another useful column to sort on is the files' size; you'll find yourself doing this a lot if you're trying to track down what huge files are gobbling up all your disk space:

```
Silver:~ btiemann$ ls -lS Desktop/
total 44812
-rw-r--r--  34367263 Aug 20 01:35 Alaska.kmz
-rw-r--r--   8012565 Jan 21 16:01 Skydive.mp4
-rw-r--r--   3191015 Jan 14 16:36 Red Rain.mp3
-rw-r--r--    139838 Jan 13 18:50 dogcookie.jpg
-rw-r--r--    126702 Dec 27 15:46 fries.gif
-rw-r--r--     10682 Dec  6 14:40 comics.rtf
```

Again, you can reverse the order of the listing with the ls -lSr command, thus putting the largest files on the bottom.

Express File Sizes in Terms of Kilo/Mega/Gigabytes

```
ls -h
```

One problem with the Unix environment is that its raw, unfiltered view of your data and its statistics often presents it in a way that's not very readable. The file sizes in the preceding examples, like 34367263, don't even do you the courtesy of adding commas, so you have to count off digits in groups of three to see if this is a file that takes up tens or hundreds of megabytes.

What's more, a megabyte (despite the metric-sounding name) isn't exactly 1000 kilobytes; it's 1024, which is a number much better suited to the binary nature of computing (1024 is 2^{10}) than the decimal 1000. Similarly, a kilobyte is 1024 bytes. This concession to computers' convenience at the expense of our own expectations means that you have to do a little mental calculation when seeing a number like 34367263, and know that it's not 34 megabytes—it's actually more like 32.

NOTE: This bit of trivia is part of why the hard drives you buy never seem to have quite as much space as was advertised on the box. It's partially because some space is inevitably lost to overhead in formatting, but it's also because hard drive manufacturers sneakily use the metric (for example, 1000×) interpretation of "mega" and "giga" to come up with the capacity they print on the box, which results in a larger number. Your Mac, however, is using the computer-ese (1024×) version, which brings the number down by a few percent. Oh, what a world....

Computers are supposed to make our lives easier, though, aren't they? Darn right they are. And they do, if we just know what commands to give them. The one you want here is -h, which expresses file sizes in friendlier terms:

```
Silver:~ btiemann$ ls -lSh Desktop/
total 44812
-rw-r--r--   32M Aug 20 01:35 Alaska.kmz
-rw-r--r--    7M Jan 21 16:01 Skydive.mp4
-rw-r--r--    3M Jan 14 16:36 Red Rain.mp3
-rw-r--r--  136K Jan 13 18:50 dogcookie.jpg
-rw-r--r--  123K Dec 27 15:46 fries.gif
-rw-r--r--   10K Dec  6 14:40 comics.rtf
```

Ah, now that's more like it!

TIP: If you find yourself typing a certain kind of ls command a lot, you might want to make an alias for it. For example, you might want to make the ll command an alias for ls -laFh, which shows all files, formats the sizes nicely, and tags folders and other special files with trailing symbols. Refer to Chapter 2 for instructions on creating aliases.

Find Out What Folder You're In

pwd

Now that you know how to list files in a folder, it's time to look at moving around through your folder tree like you're accustomed to doing graphically in the Finder.

In the standard Terminal shell in Mac OS X, your prompt tells you what folder you're in at all times:

```
Silver:~ btiemann$ cd Desktop/
Silver:~/Desktop btiemann$
```

Remember that the tilde (~) symbol is shorthand in Unix for the path to your Home directory, so this means I started in my Home directory (/Users/btiemann) and then changed to the Desktop subdirectory (/Users/btiemann/Desktop).

You might not always want to have to mentally substitute in the full absolute path when reading your prompt, or you might have changed your prompt's format so it no longer shows you your working directory. If that's the case, you can always show where you are by using the pwd (print working directory) command:

```
Silver:~/Desktop btiemann$ pwd
/Users/btiemann/Desktop
```

Change to a Different Folder

`cd`

As you saw in the previous example, you use the cd (change directory) command to move from one directory to another, the equivalent of double-clicking a folder in the Finder.

The argument that you give to cd can be an absolute path (/Users/btiemann/Documents), a relative path (~btiemann/Documents), or the name of a directory inside the current one, as in the example for the pwd command. You can also use the .. directory name to move up one level, generally the equivalent of using the Back button in the Finder:

```
Silver:~ btiemann/Desktop btiemann$ cd ..
Silver:~ btiemann$
```

TIP: You can use as many concatenated instances of .. as you want; for example, cd ../../.. will take you up three levels.

Change to the Folder You're Viewing in the Finder

Suppose you're working in a Finder window, viewing some files, and you realize you want to edit one of them in a command-line editor such as vi, or you want to quickly list its contents with a pager (such as less) without opening it up in a fully graphical application. If the folder you're in is buried deep down in your folder structure, it can be a pain to navigate your way there using cd commands.

But hey—this is a Mac. Not only is it designed to be pleasant to use on the Finder level, that level is also tightly integrated with the Terminal in ways you might not even expect. At the top of each Finder window, next to its title, is an icon representing that window's folder. Click and drag that icon into your Terminal window, and the full path of that folder will be printed into your command line.

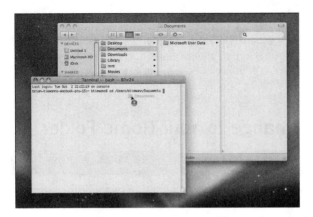

Figure 4.1 Dragging a folder's path from the Finder
into the Terminal command line.

You can, in fact, drag any folder or file into the
Terminal, and its complete path will be printed into
whatever command you're typing—be it less, cd, open,
or anything else (see Figure 4.1).

Open a Folder in the Finder

open

What about the reverse operation? Can you take a
folder you're viewing in the shell and open it in the
Finder?

Of course you can, using the open command. Simply
give it, as an argument, the name of the folder you
want to open, either as an absolute or a relative path.
You can even use the .. (parent folder) and . (current
folder) symbols:

```
Silver:~ btiemann$ open .
```

> **TIP:** The open command can be used on anything, not just folders. Opening a regular file using this command opens it in its default opener application, the same as if you'd double-clicked it in the Finder.

Change to Your Home Folder

```
cd ~
```

The Finder gives you all kinds of methods for getting to your Home folder. You can press ⌘+N, or choose **New Finder Window** from the **File** menu (provided you haven't reconfigured your Finder to open new windows elsewhere); you can choose **Home** from the **Go** menu; or you can click the icon for your Home folder in the Sidebar of any open Finder window. And that's just in the default configuration—you can create any number of other shortcuts, such as adding your Home folder to your Dock. Simple though these options might be, the sheer number of them can create its own confusion.

By comparison, the Unix way of getting back home is perhaps the simplest command of all: cd, without any arguments or options at all.

```
Silver:~/Documents/Taxes btiemann$ cd
Silver:~ btiemann$
```

If you really must have an argument (hey, maybe you're the argumentative type), you can use cd ~, which uses the tilde to specify your Home folder explicitly as the destination. It's not required, though.

Create a New Folder

`mkdir`

Making a new folder is a little bit different in the shell from in the Finder. You might be used to the Finder way, in which you press Shift+⌘+N or choose **File, New Folder**, creating a new folder in whatever window you're working in; then you type a name for the folder over the automatically selected untitled folder. In Unix, it's a one-step process: You use the mkdir (make directory) command, followed by the name of the folder, including its complete path if it's to be created anywhere but in the current directory:

```
Silver:~/Documents/Taxes btiemann$ mkdir 2006
Silver:~ biemann$ mkdir ~/Pictures/Alaska
```

If the directory you specify already exists, the command will return an error.

TIP: You can create as many directories as you want all at once; just specify all their names one after another on the command line, separated by spaces.

Newly created directories by default get the permissions string drwxr-xr-x, meaning that anybody can open and view the directory's contents, but only you are allowed to modify anything in it. If you want to make a directory private—so that other users on the same Mac can't view anything in it, even their filenames—you can change its permissions as described in Chapter 7.

TIP: The Finder has handy Back and Forward buttons that let you browse through your folder navigation history. This same functionality exists in the CLI, using the commands pushd and popd instead of cd.

Use pushd in place of cd to move into a new directory, and it adds that directory to a history "stack". Do this as many times as you like as you navigate. Then, the popd command acts like a Back button, returning you to the last location in the stack.

Create a New Series of Embedded Folders

```
mkdir -p
```

Have you ever found yourself needing to create a whole path of folders all at once—a folder inside a folder inside a folder? This isn't a particularly straightforward task either in the Finder (creating folder after folder and assigning names after the fact) or in the shell (creating each subdirectory, then changing into it and creating the next one). There's a shortcut, though, that might come in handy: mkdir -p. This command creates the entire path to the specified directory all at once, faster than even the Finder could do it.

```
Silver:~/Pictures btiemann$ mkdir -p
Vacations/2005/Alaska/Day01
```

After issuing this command, you'll find that you can cd into the Day01 folder, the Alaska folder, or the 2005 or Vacations folders—even if they hadn't existed beforehand. This isn't likely to be a command you'll use every day, but on those times when you do have a need for it, you'll sure be glad it's there.

Duplicate a File

Apple is careful to use the term *duplicate* when talking about making a brand-new copy of an existing file, rather than *copy*, a word that has some confusing double meanings. For example, you might use a Xerox machine to copy a piece of paper, making a fresh new instance of the original; but you also might copy some text into your computer's Clipboard memory so that you can paste it into another application. Apple wants you to think of *copy* in the latter sense, the cut/copy/paste sense. When you're talking about making two of something, that's *duplicating*. Hence the **File, Duplicate** command (and ⌘+D shortcut) in the Finder. That's meant to eliminate the confusion over whether "copying" a file means making two of the same thing or just saving a snapshot of the file's data that you can then paste somewhere else later.

The makers of Unix, however, weren't a part of that discussion (indeed, they predated it by a decade or more). Thus, the command that you use in the shell for making a duplicate of an existing file is, in fact, cp— which stands for *copy*.

The basic form of the cp command is to take a "source" file and duplicate it to a "destination" file, both of whose names are specified as arguments:

```
Silver:~/Pictures btiemann$ cp Banzai.jpg
BanzaiAtShow.jpg
```

You'll then find that the new file, BanzaiAtShow.jpg in this example, has been created in the same directory as

the original, with the same size and permissions, but
with its last-modified time set to the time when you
issued the command, as shown in this excerpt from
a ls -l listing:

```
-rw-r--r--  139838 Jan 13 18:50 Banzai.jpg
-rw-r--r--  139838 Feb  4 16:33 BanzaiAtShow.jpg
```

Suppose you want everything from the old file preserved in the new file, including the last-modified
stamp. That's what the -p option does: It preserves all
attributes.

```
Silver:~/Pictures btiemann$ cp -p Banzai.jpg
➥BanzaiAtShow.jpg
-rw-r--r--  139838 Jan 13 18:50 Banzai.jpg
-rw-r--r--  139838 Jan 13 18:50 BanzaiAtShow.jpg
```

TIP: You can specify complete paths for either the
source or destination files. This allows you to duplicate
a file from your current directory into some completely
different directory, or vice versa.

Duplicate Files Extra Safely

```
cp -i
```

Notice that there was no warning about the
BanzaiAtShow.jpg file already existing. That's because
the cp command doesn't normally check to see if
there's a file with the same name as the destination you
specified; it overwrites it automatically and silently. This
can be pretty dangerous. You might think it won't

affect you, but every Unix veteran has horror stories about accidentally trashing important files by copying other files over them. One way to prevent this from happening is with the -i (interactive) option:

```
Silver:~/Pictures btiemann$ cp -i Banzai.jpg
➥BanzaiAtShow.jpg
overwrite BanzaiAtShow.jpg? (y/n [n]) n
not overwritten
```

Now that's a lot safer. Still, though, it's a pain to have to remember to type -i every time. If we're going to be doing that, we might as well be remembering to always check the directory contents for name conflicts, right?

Not if you make an alias! Refer back to Chapter 2 for instructions on how to make the following command alias:

```
alias cp="cp -i"
```

This changes the cp command itself to really mean cp -i, with the "safety net" feature built right in. You'll never have to worry about accidentally overwriting something important again.

TIP: You might, however, want to keep the "unsafe" version of cp around, just in case you plan to copy hundreds of files at once; otherwise, you'll get prompted for whether to overwrite every one of those hundreds of files, one at a time. To do this, make the alias called ci or something, and then remember to use that command instead of cp unless you want to live dangerously.

Duplicate Multiple Files Using Wildcards

cp *

Remember back in Chapter 3, "Using the Command Line," when you learned how to use wildcards (such as * and ?) to specify whole bunches of files all at once, matching a certain filename pattern? Well, here's where that technique starts to come in handy. Suppose you want to copy (sorry, duplicate) a few dozen photos from one folder into another—namely, all the ones whose names start with IMG_ (as Canon digital cameras tend to name them). Now, you could go into the Finder and fiddle around with the listing options until you had a block of contiguous files that you could select and then drag to another place; or, if you're in the shell, you can just use wildcards to specify them all:

```
Silver:~/Pictures/Alaska/ btiemann$ cp IMG_*
~/Desktop/Alaska_Photos
```

You can get even more specific. Suppose you wanted to copy only photos that are numbered in a certain range—IMG_5531.JPG to IMG_5536.JPG. You can do that using the [] wildcards, which specify a range of numbers or letters within brackets that match a single character:

```
Silver:~/Pictures/Alaska/ btiemann$ cp IMG_553[1-6]
~/Desktop/Alaska_Photos
```

Duplicate a Folder

```
cp -R
```

You use the cp command to duplicate folders, too, not just files. However, just using the bare cp command won't get you anywhere:

```
Silver:~/Desktop btiemann$ cp Alaska_Photos
Alaska_Photos2
cp: Alaska_Photos is a directory (not copied).
```

What you need is the -R (recursive) option, which tells cp to traverse the directory and copy all its contents as well as the folder itself:

```
Silver:~/Desktop btiemann$ cp -R Alaska_Photos
Alaska_Photos2
```

This causes a file-for-file duplication of the source directory, including all subdirectories that might be inside it.

NOTE: Be careful when specifying the target directory name. If you don't append the / character, some commands (such as cp -R) will overwrite the target directory with the one you're copying, rather than copying the contents *into* the target. The trailing / ensures that the items you're copying go *into* the target directory.

Duplicate Folders While Preserving Important File Information

cp -Rp

If you use the cp -R command to duplicate a folder, you'll notice that although all files are duplicated, they're also given brand-new last-modified dates, just like in the earlier example where you saw what happens if you copy a file without specifying the -p option. The same behavior applies here; use the -p option in conjunction with -R to duplicate a folder to a perfectly identical copy:

```
Silver:~/Desktop btiemann$ cp -Rp Alaska_Photos
Alaska_Photos2
```

This is the technique you'd want to use in backing up your files. For example, if you bought an external hard drive, you could back up your entire home directory in a single command like this:

```
Silver:~ btiemann$ cp -Rp . /Volumes/Backup\ Disk/
```

Be prepared for this process to take a long time, though—and be sure to disable your cp -i alias if you created one, or else you'll be approving every single overwrite of your previously backed-up files!

Move or Rename a File

mv

Coming from the world of the Finder, you might be used to the fact that *moving* and *renaming* files are

completely different procedures. One involves dragging
an icon from one place to another, and one involves
clicking a filename and typing a new one. But that's
the GUI way of doing things, and although it can be
more efficient if you've got a mouse available, that's
not always the case if you're typing at a command line.

Long ago, when Unix was first being written, and
nobody had yet conceived of a windowing operating
system driven by a mouse, the concepts of moving and
renaming files were very similar. Indeed, because Unix
considers a file's "name" to be its complete path (such
as /Users/btiemann/Documents/Taxes/2006/Federal.pdf),
changing its name to something like /Users/btiemann/
Desktop/2006-fed.pdf is functionally the same thing as
moving it to another location. It's still the same file; it's
just addressed using a different path and filename now.
Whether you consider this a "move" or a "rename"
operation is really a matter of philosophy.

That's why the same command is used in Unix for
both moving and renaming files: mv, short for "move."
It operates in much the same way as the cp command,
taking a source and a destination name and changing
the specified file or directory to the specified destination name, whether it's in the same directory as the
first one or not.

```
Silver:~ btiemann$ mv
Documents/Taxes/2006/Federal.pdf Desktop/2006-
fed.pdf
```

After issuing this command, the Federal.pdf file is no
longer to be found in the Documents/Taxes/2006 folder,
and is instead on my desktop, with the new name
2006-fed.pdf. It's been both renamed and moved at the
same time.

You can move a file without renaming it, and you can rename a file without moving it; both of these are degenerate cases of the example you just saw. For instance:

```
Silver:~ btiemann$ mv 2006-fed.pdf Documents
```

This moves the file into my Documents folder, just as if I'd dragged it there in the Finder. And I can rename it by simply placing myself in the same folder as the file and specifying a destination name that's also in the same folder:

```
Silver:~ btiemann$ cd Documents
Silver:~/Documents btiemann$ mv 2006-fed.pdf 2006-
1040.pdf
```

See how that works? Without a mouse and a GUI to insulate you from the nuts and bolts of how the underlying operating system thinks of files, these operations are so similar in nature that there's really no point in having separate commands for renaming and moving items.

And now, congratulations: You're officially part of an elite group who thinks it's perfectly logical to use a command called "mv" to rename a file. Your mother will never understand you again.

TIP: The mv command works on directorie   s the same as it does on files. Because all you're doing is changing the name and location of the folder itself, there's no need to worry about recursion or preserving file attributes; you just move or rename the folder, and everything in it stays the same as it was. That's also why mv is much faster than cp. Rather than making dozens of duplicates and deleting them, it's just changing the Unix name of a single item.

NOTE: The same caution applies to mv as to cp: It doesn't warn you if you're moving or renaming something to a destination that already exists, and you'll overwrite it if you are. You can use the -i option to make mv warn you and prompt for confirmation if there's a name collision, but just as with cp, you'll have to decide for yourself whether it's worth it to make it part of the standard mv command with an alias, knowing that it'll also trip you up if you try to move lots of files at once.

Delete a File

    rm

If you're used to DOS, you might have found yourself typing commands like dir and del and copy, expecting them to work the same way in Unix as they do in DOS. Although many of the DOS command names do make more sense in some ways than the terse little two-letter commands like ls and cp and mv, they won't work in the Mac OS X shell, which harks back to an earlier authority—the same one that decided that rm ("remove") should be the command for deleting files, not del.

Removing files is an instantaneous operation: if you delete a file with rm, it's gone. There is no inherent equivalent of the Trash can that you see in your Mac's Dock. Whereas in the traditional Mac way of doing things you first drag unwanted items into the Trash and then you empty the Trash at some later point

when it's getting too full, in the shell you simply rm a
file and then just hope you don't ever need it again.

TIP: Just because the shell doesn't have a built-in
Trash doesn't mean you can't take advantage of the
one in your Dock. Instead of using rm to delete files
immediately, try simply moving them to the hidden
.Trash folder in your Home directory, which is the
shell's representation of the Trash can:

```
Silver:~/Documents btiemann$ mv junkfile.pdf
~/.Trash
```

Then you can empty the Trash at a later date, just as
you normally would with files you put there using the
Finder (choose **Finder, Empty Trash**).

To use rm, give it the name of the file you want to
delete (or a list of files separated by spaces):

```
Silver:~/Documents btiemann$ rm junkfile.pdf
```

Do an ls now and you'll find that junkfile.pdf is no
longer there—and you're not likely to get it back,
either. Always use the rm command with the utmost
caution!

Delete Multiple Files Using Wildcards

```
rm *
```

As easy as it is to shoot yourself in the foot using rm,
Unix makes it even easier by allowing you to specify
wildcards, just as in cp and mv and most other commands. For example, suppose you want to get rid of all

the digital photos that start with IMG_ in your Pictures directory:

```
Silver:~/Pictures btiemann$ rm IMG_*
```

Wow, that was easy. Almost too easy, huh? Just a thought, but—maybe mv IMG_* ~/.Trash might be a safer idea.

Delete Files Extra Safely

```
rm -i
```

There are all kinds of ways to make rm even more dangerous, and the only reason I'm bringing them up now is to make sure you think about them every time you find yourself even typing "r" and "m" close together. For example, if you meant to type rm *.jpg and instead typed rm * .jpg (with a space), you'd end up deleting *all* files in that directory, not just the JPEG ones.

Everybody's made mistakes and deleted important files unintentionally. One way to defend against that—that is, if you insist on using rm rather than just moving things to ~/.Trash—is to use the -i (interactive) option, which works the same as in cp and mv:

```
Silver:~/Documents btiemann$ rm -i junkfile.pdf
remove junkfile.pdf? y
```

As with the previous commands that support the -i option, you can set up a safety net by aliasing rm -i to rm (see Chapter 2), but it's going to get in your way if you ever have to delete a whole bunch of files all at once. It's probably a good idea to go ahead and set up the alias, though, because being prompted for confirmation on every one of several dozen files is a good reason for you to move them to ~/.Trash rather than trying to delete them outright.

Delete a Folder

```
rm -Rf
```

The way to delete a folder in the shell, or at least the one you're going to be the most interested in, is the rm -Rf command (the -R option deletes recursively, and the -f option is a "force" flag that tells rm not to bother prompting you if it runs into files or folders that can't be deleted because they belong to someone else or aren't empty).

```
Silver:~/Documents btiemann$ rm -Rf OldJunk
```

The alert reader (that's you) will have noticed, though, that this is potentially really, really dangerous, especially if you start messing around with wildcards at the same time as recursive deletion with the safety switched off. Essentially what it's going to do is delete everything in the tree below the point you specify, and it won't even stop to ask directions.

This gets even hairier when you realize that if you consider the .. directory to be "inside" the current directory, then a recursive delete operation can even move *up* the directory tree if you specify a file list that includes it. To illustrate: Once I was trying to get rid of all the hidden files in a user's Home directory (those are the ones that begin with a dot, like .profile and .bash_history). So what did I do? Why, I cleverly entered rm -Rf .*. And what do you suppose it did? That's right—after deleting everything in the current directory, it immediately traversed up to the parent level (following the .., which my command matched), and started deleting everything in that directory (which included other users' Home folders). Then it moved up another level, and another, until it got to the top of the system and proceeded to delete every last item in the system until even the rm command had been deleted. All from one simple, 10-letter command.

Now, it isn't necessarily going to be that bad. My total meltdown experience came about because I was running as root, which essentially means that file permissions are irrelevant to me; this kind of thing can't be easily done in Mac OS X, where there is no root account and all administrative actions must be done through sudo, which we'll discuss a little later. But such a command will still traverse the entire system's directory tree, and it'll delete everything that it's permitted to, which includes any applications or system extensions that you've ever installed. In short, no matter how many safeguards you have in place, a flubbed recursive rm command with wildcards is virtually guaranteed to ruin the rest of your day.

NOTE: There is a command in Unix intended for deleting empty directories: rmdir. You can use this command if you're absolutely sure the directory is empty—for instance, if you just created it and now realize that you don't need it. But in Mac OS X, there's virtually no chance you'll ever encounter a folder that's truly empty, because if you ever so much as change the folder's window size in the Finder, there's a .DS_Store file that gets created (which stores information about how the folder is viewed). If you try to use rmdir on a folder with anything at all in it, including .DS_Store, it will fail. For this reason, you might as well just consider rm -Rf the command for deleting folders.

Delete Troublesome Files

Sooner or later, there will come a time when you've
got a file that you need to delete, and for whatever
reason—usually because something's screwy with the
filename—you just can't seem to delete it using the
normal rm command. You have to be able to specify
the filename on the command line—rm *filename*—
and sometimes you won't be able to type a filename
properly, the way it appears in the Finder.

Björk

Figure 4.2 A filename that's difficult to type on the
command line.

Figure 4.2 shows a folder with a name that I entered
using the Mac's excellent special-character-typing
mechanism, which you'll learn more about in
Chapter 6, "Viewing and Editing Text Files." (To
make the ö character, I pressed Option+U to create
the umlaut combining character and then pressed
O to combine it with the umlaut.) But that mechanism doesn't work in the Terminal; if you use that
sequence of keys at the shell, it performs a mysterious and undocumented operation that only results in
whatever key you press being entered six times. That's
clearly not what you want, and it leaves you high and
dry if the command you're trying to type is rm -Rf
Björk. So what do you do?

NOTE: If you list the current directory's contents, the folder that looks so well-behaved in Figure 4.2 looks like this:

    Bjo??rk

Those sequences of question marks, if you see them on the command line, indicate files whose names you're not likely to be able to type directly.

There's a number of possibilities you can try. The first is to rely on the bash shell's handy Tab completion feature. Type **rm -Rf Bj** and then press Tab:

```
Silver:~/Desktop btiemann$ rm -Rf Bjo\314\210rk/
```

Interesting! It has automatically filled in the command with escaped octal codes for the Unicode character ö. If you press Return, the command will execute normally, deleting the directory just as you expect. So you don't have to type the letter at all, as long as the shell can figure out that Bjӧrk is uniquely the file you're interested in. (If there's another file in there called Bjürk, then you've got problems.)

There are still more techniques for getting rid of files whose names you just can't address directly. One is to take advantage of the fact that if you can't address a file individually, a wildcard will still catch it:

```
Silver:~/Desktop btiemann$ rm -Rf Bj?rk
```

Or you can create a temporary folder, move all the files in the current directory into the new folder, and then move all the files *except* for the troublesome one back out again. Then delete the whole temporary folder.

Other problems can arise if a file contains characters that you can type, but that interacts oddly with the rm command itself. You saw in Chapter 3 how to deal with files whose names have spaces and other non-alphanumeric characters in them: Put a backslash (\) in front of them to make the shell treat them literally, and not as part of the command:

```
Silver:~/Desktop btiemann$ rm Shopping\ List.txt
```

If I hadn't put the backslash in this command, the shell would have treated it as two separate arguments and tried to delete a file called Shopping and another one called List.txt. The backslash makes the space part of the filename, not of the command syntax.

Another kind of problematic file is one with a dash (-) at the front of the filename. You can't just type rm -file.txt, because any argument to rm that begins with a dash is treated as an option string:

```
Silver:~/Desktop btiemann$ rm -file.txt
rm: illegal option -- l
usage: rm [-f | -i] [-dPRrvW] file ...
➥unlink file
```

So -f and -i were valid options, but -l wasn't—and who knows about the rest of the file.txt string? Now, it seems like there isn't a good way out of this; but there is: the -- option. This is an option that turns off all subsequent options. Everything following it is treated as a literal argument:

```
Silver:~/Desktop btiemann$ rm -- -file.txt
```

That's more like it.

There's one more thing I must point out: By pointing and clicking, the Finder is almost always going to be capable of manipulating any file that appears in the filesystem. In the graphical layer, files aren't addressed by their names, but by database objects that are all readable to the system, and you will always be able to click and drag an item to put it in the Trash—or rename it to something more shell friendly.

Issue a Privileged Command Using sudo

If you've used Linux or other Unix variants, you're probably familiar with the concept of root, also known as the superuser. This is a special administrative user account that is immune to file access permissions; if you're logged in as root, you can do pretty much anything to any files on the system. That's why root is used for making system configuration changes, installing software, and doing other things that regular users can't do.

It's also a dangerous thing to have around. A system with a root account presents an easy way for hackers and malware to take control of it. If someone gets root access, all the data in the system is up for grabs, and there's no way to clean out the detritus of the incursion short of completely wiping and reinstalling the system.

Mac OS X doesn't have a root account that you can log in to. Rather, it operates on the sudo model, which is something that's increasing in popularity in the Linux/Unix world at large. Rather than being logged in as a user called root, you log in as yourself—and if you have to perform any action that requires privileged access, such as modifying files that don't belong to you, you precede your command with the keyword sudo (which stands for "superuser: do"). You're then prompted for your own password, and if you enter it correctly, the command is executed with root privileges.

NOTE: Prompting you for your own password ensures that the command is really being executed by you, and not just someone who came and sat down at your computer when you stepped out to get coffee. If you were logged in as root, anyone could sit down and issue any nefarious command without being challenged.

Beware, though, that sudo authorizes you to perform administrative tasks for five minutes before it prompts you again. This is a convenience, and like all convenience features, it's potentially a security risk. Don't get up and leave your computer until five minutes after your last sudo action!

Only certain users on a Mac OS X system are permitted to use sudo. Those users are the ones who are identified as Admin users in the Accounts pane of the System Preferences. Standard users are not allowed to use sudo commands. For this reason, as the administrator of your Mac, you should be careful about which accounts you create with Admin privileges; if it's a shared household computer or a lab machine, don't give Admin privileges to anyone you don't trust not to install harmful software, fiddle with system settings, or read other users' sensitive data, because all those things are possible for Admin users.

In the GUI of Mac OS X, a dialog box automatically pops up to ask for your password if a privileged action (such as changing TCP/IP settings or installing software into /Applications) is requested, as shown in Figure 4.3.

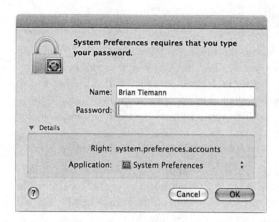

Figure 4.3 Mac OS X prompting for authentication upon performing a privileged action.

In the Details section, you can see what the name of the access right is that's being requested (here, it's the "accounts" subsection of "preferences," which is part of "system") and what application is requesting it (System Preferences). This lets you always be aware of what changes are being made to your system, and see that they're changes you explicitly asked for and authorized.

The difference between the GUI and CLI versions of sudo, though, is that in the CLI you're able to issue any command you want with administrative privileges. In the GUI, there are only certain things you can do that require administrative access, such as running installers and changing system settings. But in the CLI, anything you precede with sudo—no matter how crazy—will be executed with complete disregard for the system's access privileges—so be careful!

```
Silver:~ btiemann$ sudo ls ~joeuser/Pictures/
```

Later in this book you'll see a few examples of system settings you can change by editing files in the /etc directory, which are generally owned by root and thus aren't editable by you except through sudo. To modify these files, you'll launch a text editor using sudo:

```
Silver:~ btiemann$ sudo pico /etc/resolv.conf
```

This enables the editor to save the root-owned file even though it wasn't really root who opened it. That's the essence of system administration in Mac OS X. It's a little more cumbersome than simply entering the commands you want to run while logged in as the all-powerful root, but it's also far safer.

CAUTION: Always remember that the whole point of restricting access to privileged commands is to protect the system and its data! The sudo command can be used to perform destructive or invasive actions (such as deleting critical system files or looking at other users' private data) just as it can be used for legitimate configuration and administration. Don't do anything through sudo unless you're confident you know what will happen!

Read About a Command with man

man

Unix does have a help system. Okay, it's not as well organized or easy to read or well illustrated as the Help in the graphical portion of Mac OS X, but it's likely to be a lot more indispensable in your daily computing. It's called man, the *manual*.

Every command in the Mac OS X shell has a man page. This page is a browsable file that contains all the options you can give to the command, all the possibilities of its syntax, and all the expected results. For example, if you wanted to find out about all the options that you can give the ls command, including the ones not covered in this book, enter the following:

```
Silver:~ btiemann$ man ls
```

This brings up the man page for ls in the less pager, which you'll learn more about in Chapter 6.

```
LS(1)     BSD General Commands Manual LS(1)
NAME
     ls -- list directory contents
SYNOPSIS
     ls [-ABCFGHLPRTWZabcdefghiklmnopqrstuwx1]
       [file ...]
DESCRIPTION
     For each operand that names a file of a type
other than directory, ls displays its name as well
as any requested, associated information.  For each
operand that names a file of type directory, ls dis-
plays the names of files contained within that
directory, as well as any requested, associated
information.
     If no operands are given, the contents of the
current directory are displayed.  If more than one
operand is given, non-directory operands are dis-
played first; directory and non-directory operands
are sorted separately and in lexicographical order.
     The following options are available:
     -A       List all entries except for . and ...
       Always set for the super-
:
```

The man page starts out with formalized headers: the name of the command (along with its short description as used by apropos, as you'll see in the next section), its synopsis (basic syntax model), and description. It's then followed by details of all the options. There's a lot more to the page, as you can see from the colon at the bottom. In the less pager, that means you can scroll down using the down-arrow key one line at a time or using the spacebar to move down one page at a time. You can also move up with the up arrow, or up a page using the W key.

To quit out of the man page, press Q.

Search for More Commands Based on Function

The manual is great for looking up more information on a command that you already know exists. But what if you want to perform a certain function, but you don't know what the command for it is? That's where the apropos command comes in.

Suppose you want to find out about commands that deal with speech, such as in text-to-speech generation (you want to have your Mac read a text file aloud). You'd enter the following command:

```
Silver:~ btiemann$ apropos speech
```

The system searches a database of keywords found in the NAME section of each command's man page and returns a list of all the relevant commands where a match to your search string was found:

```
Mac::Speech(3pm)          - Provide interface to
                            PlainTalk (Speech
                            Manager)
say(1)                    - Convert text to audible
                            speech
```

Aha! There's a command called say, which seems to do exactly what you're looking for.

NOTE: The number in parentheses indicates what section of the manual the command's documentation is found in. You'd need to worry about this only if the command appeared in more than one section of the manual, in which case you'd have to specify the section in the man command: **man 5 crontab.**

You can now use man to look up more information about the command, such as its proper syntax and options. This is how you'll learn about all the commands available to you on the Unix side of the Force.

```
Silver:~ btiemann$ man say
```

Conclusion

This is by far the longest chapter of this book, and with good reason: It's an attempt to cram all the basic building blocks of Unix into a single whirlwind tour. There's a great deal more to the command environment than what's been covered here, such as data flow control, input/output streams, basic shell programming with conditional execution, and so on. These kinds of advanced techniques, although useful for hard-core Unix-heads, aren't likely to be all that important to you as a Mac user; this book's goal is to introduce you to the cool stuff you can do *with your Mac* that you might not otherwise know about—not to focus on the nitty-gritty of the Unix core to the exclusion of what's uniquely "Mac" about your computer. You can always learn more about Unix in any of its myriad forms from a much thicker book; but we've got limited space here, and so we'd better move on to what you can do with the graphical Finder.

## 5

Using the Finder

It can be fun to poke around at the Unix command line, but let's be honest—the reason why you got a Mac wasn't so you could use Unix. If that's what you were after, you could have just installed Linux for free on a cheap PC.

No—the Unix underpinnings of Mac OS X are neat, and they can be really useful to delve into directly, but they're only a small part of what makes the Mac what it is. The majority of the cool tricks you're going to discover as a Mac user are, in fact, things you can do in the GUI layer, the part of the system that everybody's used to seeing. It's designed to be a flexible and tweak-able interface to your data, just like the Unix layer is— and there's plenty more you can do with a mouse than with a keyboard alone.

The place to start looking at the Mac OS X GUI is the Finder, the built-in filesystem navigator.

Files, Folders, Aliases, and Bundles

In Chapter 3, "Using the Command Line," you learned that as far as Unix is concerned, every discrete piece of data in the system is a "file"—the only thing distinguishing an image file from a directory or a device handle or a network socket is an identifier stored with the file, and most Unix commands work the same way on all files.

In the graphical layer, though, there's quite a bit more complexity. Different types of files that function differently all have their own distinct icons, behaviors, and default actions for when you double-click them. Indeed, certain kinds of files that appear more or less equivalent to each other in the Unix level of the system are quite a bit different in the Finder.

Regular files and folders operate in pretty much the way you might expect. Different file types receive different icons, depending on what applications they're affiliated with, and some files' icons can display previews of their contents (most notably, image files, although in Column view you can also get live previews of movie files and text documents in the rightmost column). Folders all share the same icons (except for the special organizational ones at the top of your Home folder, like Pictures, Movies, and Documents) and behave the same way, and can be navigated in the Finder using any of three modes: Icon view, List view, and Column view. The type of view mode you select, as well as the shape, size, and position of the folder's window, are saved when you close the window, and it opens in that same position and with the same shape the next time you open the folder's Finder window.

TIP: Mac traditionalists and user-interface purists often criticize the Mac OS X Finder for its lack of "spatiality," meaning that folders aren't always guaranteed to pop open into independent windows with their positions and sizes just the way you set them, like they did in the old days. Mac OS X allows that a folder whose icon you double-click from within another folder window will open into the existing window, its contents replacing the parent folder's, and the window's dimensions not changing. If you want to ensure spatiality, turn on the **Always open folders in a new window** option in the Finder Preferences (it's off by default). It's not perfect— it doesn't ensure that only one copy of a folder window can be open at once, for example—but it can help. (You can also hold down the ⌘ key as you double-click a folder to open it in an independent window.)

TIP: You can apply custom icons to any files or folders you choose. First copy an image into memory by pressing ⌘+C (either in a graphics program or by selecting the icon in the **File, Get Info** palette on a file whose icon you want to copy from); then open the **Get Info** palette on the file whose icon you want to change, select the icon, and press ⌘+V to paste it.

You can make your own custom icon sets using shareware tools such as Iconographer (http://www.mscape.com/).

The Finder supports *aliases*, (not to be confused with the command-line aliases you learned about in Chapter 2) which are like the shortcuts in Windows and symbolic links in Unix; they're pointers to other items that can exist anywhere else on your disk. Aliases are great for streamlining your productivity while allowing you to keep your data organized. You can keep a commonly accessed file in your Documents folder and have an alias to it sitting on your desktop so you can get to it easily.

Aliases are actually more like shortcuts in Windows than the Unix symbolic links you'll encounter later in this chapter. They're richer in content, with the capability to keep track of the location of the target item even if you move it from one folder to another. An

alias can even know that its target is to be found on a
network volume and dial your modem and mount the
volume automatically if you try to access the item.
Symlinks, by contrast, are very sparse Unix entities that
contain nothing but a name and a path to the target's
location, which can get broken if you move the target.
Aliases you create in the Finder appear as regular files
if you look at them on the command line, because
really that's what they are—files that act like symlinks
when executed by the Finder. However, symlinks that
you create at the command line look and work like
aliases if you view them in the Finder: You see an icon
that's cloned from the target item, with a curved arrow
in the corner, and double-clicking it opens the target
item. Deleting an alias or a symlink doesn't do anything to the target item.

Files, folders, and aliases probably aren't anything new
to you if you've got even a passing familiarity with
Windows, Linux, or the Mac. What you might not be
familiar with, though, are *bundles*. These are a feature
that's unique to Mac OS X (and its predecessor,
NeXTSTEP/OpenStep): folders, packed full of data,
that act like monolithic files when you encounter
them in the Finder. A bundle can be opened and
examined, but only if you issue a special command in
the Finder (as you'll see later in this chapter); otherwise, it just looks like a plain old file. But if you look
at a bundle in the Unix command line, it appears as a
directory, the same as any other folder in the system.

Mac OS X usually creates bundles automatically as
a means of saving certain file types. If you create a
text document in TextEdit and you throw in a few
images, for instance, the file you save isn't an RTF

document—it's actually an RTF Directory, with the extension .rtfd, that contains your file's plain text and the embedded images as separate items. Yet it all looks and acts like a single neat file.

Applications in Mac OS X are bundles, too. An application is a bundle with the hidden .app extension, whose contents include executable binaries for one or more system architectures (Intel and PowerPC, for example), as well as resource files containing the app's text strings, bitmap images, and sound-effect files. When you double-click the icon for an application, Mac OS X looks inside the bundle, finds the appropriate executable for your system, and launches it. All you know is that you double-clicked a neat little icon; you never have to know about all the libraries and resources packed away underneath it. This is what helps keep your Applications folder so much neater-looking than the Program Files folder in Windows, to say nothing of the /usr/bin and /usr/local/bin litany you find in Unix.

NOTE: Many applications also save their data files as bundles. iMovie, for example, stores all its working video clips in the folder structure within the bundle. That way, gigabytes of movie data, which you generally don't need to see in the Finder, are all gathered under a single icon with a .iMovieProject filename.

You probably won't ever have to worry about creating bundles on your own, unless you're an application developer. But even so, it's good to know how they operate, and—as you'll see later—how to dig into them if necessary.

Customize Icon View

View → Show View Options
⌘+J

Icon view, like the standard output of the `ls` command, is pretty sparse by default, but it can be spruced up through the liberal application of view options. These options can be accessed by viewing a Finder window in Icon view (click the leftmost of the three view icons) and then choosing **View, Show View Options** (or pressing ⌘+J).

Icons can be any size you want, from 16×16 pixels up to 128×128. Very large icons can be useful in folders full of images, especially if you've got the **Show icon preview** option enabled, which replaces the file's icon with a thumbnail of its contents.

Similarly, in Mac OS X 10.5 (Leopard) and later, there's a **Grid spacing** slider that lets you adjust how far apart your icons are spaced when automatically arranged on the grid.

The **Show item info** option places a small string under the filename showing key data about the file's contents, depending on the item type. Folders show how many items are enclosed, image files show their pixel dimensions, and movie and audio files show their length.

The other options are pretty much self-explanatory; feel free to experiment with label text size and placement, grid layout, and arrangement order. Setting the background to a color or an image brings up a picker that lets you specify the color or image to use; bear in mind, though, that an image you select as the background can't be thrown away or the folder will revert to white. You also can't adjust the text size or tiling behavior of the background image, unfortunately.

TIP: If you don't enable the **Snap to grid** option, you can still keep your icons neatly lined up using the **View, Clean Up** command, which moves icons to their nearest grid location. Similarly, you can use the **View, Arrange By** command to sort your icons by the criterion you choose. Bear in mind, though, that the **Arrange By** view option doesn't wipe out your custom icon placements—if you turn the option off later, the icons will move back to where you'd originally put them.

Finally, at the bottom of the palette is a button labeled **Use as Defaults**. Unless you click this button, the adjustments you make to the window's icon arrangement apply only to this window and no others. Clicking the button applies the same settings to all other folder windows that don't have their own custom settings applied.

NOTE: Prior to Mac OS X 10.5 (Leopard), the first option in the palette is a choice between **This window only** or **All windows**. Make sure you're working in the proper context before making any adjustments, or else you might find that you've accidentally changed the entire system's settings when you'd only meant to adjust one folder.

Customize List View

View → Show View Options
⌘+J

List view, the second of the three view icons, gives you a file listing similar to the `ls -l` view you saw at the command line. You'll have less control over how the files are arranged and how their icons appear than in Icon view, but far more information about what's in them. Up to seven informational columns can be shown along with each file, in whatever order you want, and the configuration can be applied per folder or as a global default, the same as with Icon view.

NOTE: Although they look different from the [+] junctions of the Windows Explorer's tree view, Mac OS X's disclosure arrows work the same way: Click one to turn it down and reveal a folder's contents in an indented list. What doesn't work the same as in Windows, though, is the sort order. Folders on the Mac are sorted alphabetically along with the rest of the files, rather than being listed first before all files.

Most of the view options in List view are pretty straightforward in meaning. You can pick from two icon sizes and seven text sizes, and you can specify which of the available info columns are presented. When viewing a Finder window, you can sort the files on any column by clicking its header, and reverse the sort order by clicking it again. Drag column headers left and right to change the order in which they're listed.

The last two view options in the palette are a little more obscure: **Use relative dates**, if enabled, allows the Finder to list items that were last modified today or yesterday as "Today" or "Yesterday," rather than with their full date strings. **Calculate all sizes** is an option you should enable only if you've got a fast computer or a lot of time on your hands. It ensures that folders in List view are listed along with their cumulative sizes, which requires Mac OS X to sum up everything inside each folder as soon as you scroll to it, which can cause serious lag problems if there are a lot of subfolders to dig through. Enable this option only on a per-window basis, not as a global policy!

TIP: Widen or narrow the info columns by dragging the edges of the column headers. As you narrow the **Date Modified** or **Date Created** columns, the format of the date changes to better fit the available space.

You can change the format of the date to suit your taste. Open up the System Preferences and go to the **Formats** section of the **International** pane, and click **Customize** in either the **Dates** or **Times** section to manually put together the date and time format you like from basic components.

Get Detailed File Info

File → Get Info
⌘+I

Column view, the third of the three view icons, is the least customizable of the view modes (all you can adjust is the text size and whether the icons and the preview column are shown); but it's also the quickest means of navigating through the filesystem hierarchy without rich file info or icon arrangement slowing you down. In Column view, each click of a folder opens up a new column with that folder's contents to the right. Keep clicking until you reach the file you want, select it, and a preview of that file—with many key details, such as the kind, size, and dates of last modification, creation, and the last time it was opened— appears in the final column. There's also a button labeled **More Info**. This button opens a panel hence-forth referred to as the Get Info panel, because the

more direct and universal way to access it is by selecting an item—in any view mode—and then choosing
the **File, Get Info** command.

The Get Info panel consists of some basic information
and the file's icon at the top, followed by seven col-
lapsible sections:

- **Spotlight Comments**—Any text you type in
  here becomes searchable keywords that let you
  find the file quickly through Spotlight, the systemwide search mechanism, accessible through
  the magnifying-glass icon in the top-right corner
  or in any Finder window.

- **General**—This section contains the same informational fields that are available in the Column
  view preview column, plus a color label that you
  can set (to help you distinguish in-progress projects from completed ones, and so on), and two
  extra options that are seldom used, but useful to
  know about.

  - The **Stationery Pad** option, if enabled, tells
    the Finder that if you double-click the file
    rather than opening the file directly in its open-
    er application, it should first duplicate the file—
    creating a clone with the word "(copy)"
    appended to its name—and open *that* file in the
    opener app. This can be useful if you want a file
    to behave as a template, ensuring that it won't
    itself be overwritten with new changes.

  - The **Open using Rosetta** option, which is
    available only on applications, tells the Finder to
    launch the app using the Rosetta code-transla-
    tion environment, which simulates a PowerPC
    architecture on an Intel-based Mac. This option

is rarely useful except to developers, but some apps newly ported to Intel might have to be launched under Rosetta to run properly.

- The **Locked** option makes a file read-only. If you're the owner of the file, you can override the lock at the time you save changes to it; but otherwise it can't be altered. This option is an artifact of the days before Mac OS X's Unix underpinnings and its true multiuser permissions architecture, and you can probably safely ignore it—it has essentially the same effect as setting the Permissions to Read-Only.

- **More Info**—This contains information fields specific to the file type. Plain-text files might have only the last-opened date; but other types, such as digital photos, might have a dozen or so additional fields, from pixel dimensions to the camera manufacturer, model, and focal length.

- **Name & Extension**—The complete filename lives here, along with a check box that indicates whether the extension is hidden. If you want to manipulate the filename directly without going through the Finder's layer that protects the extension-based file-typing scheme, this is the place to do it.

- **Open With**—This is where you define what application is used to open individual files or all files of a given type. You'll see more about this in Chapter 9, "Working with Applications."

- **Preview**—A 128×128 pane showing a thumbnail of an image, a playable video or audio clip, or a generic full-size icon for most other file types.

- **Languages**—A list of all the languages an application is written in. You can disable certain languages to reduce the app's memory footprint, or add more language string files that aren't already in the app's bundle.

- **Ownership & Permissions**—Full control over the Unix permissions of your files. You'll learn more about this in Chapter 7, "Ownership and Permissions."

Any changes you make in the Get Info panel are immediately applied. If you can't find some piece of information about a file, and the Unix layer doesn't give it to you, the Get Info panel is the place to go.

Create an Alias to a File or Folder

File → Make Alias
⌘+L

Creating an alias in the Finder is a pretty straightforward operation. Select the item (file, folder, application, or disk volume) you want to make an alias of, then choose **File, Make Alias**.

TIP: Most of the commands in the **File** menu of the Finder are available as contextual menu commands, also known as "right-click menu" commands. On the Mac, a right-click can be simulated by holding down the Control key as you click. Remember, too, that Mac OS X supports any multibutton USB mouse you care to install, so right-clicking for real is always an option.

The newly created alias, which you can recognize by the curved arrow in the corner of its icon (and the word "alias" on its label), can be renamed and moved to any location where it's convenient to have it. You can also move the target item anywhere you want; the alias can keep track of it by using its Unique File ID, not its absolute path. That's one strength that the Mac's HFS+ filesystem has over both the Windows and Unix worlds, which depend on pathnames for locating files.

(Don't ask me why, if you move an application that you've got in the Dock to another location, the Dock loses track of it. The Dock indexes certain things by path, which I think is stupid.)

TIP: Another way to create an alias is to hold down Option and Command (⌘) while you click and drag the target item into a different Finder window or the desktop (your pointer turns into a curved arrow when it's being used to make an alias in this way). This creates an alias that doesn't have the "alias" tag added to its label, eliminating the need to change the label manually after creating the alias.

Create a Symbolic Link

```
ln -s
```

If you have the need to link to a file or other item from a different part of the system, and you need to have the Unix layer be able to find the target item as well (for instance, if you want to share files from an aliased folder using the built-in web server, Apache, which is a Unix utility), you'll need to use a symbolic link rather than a Mac-style alias.

To create a symlink, first drop to the Terminal shell. Then use the `ln` (link) command, along with the `-s` (symbolic) option:

```
Silver:~ btiemann$ ln -s
➥Pictures/Vacation Public/VacationPhotos
```

Now the link appears in the Finder just like a regular alias, and it also functions as an alias in the Unix layer, as Unix utilities such as Apache expect it to.

NOTE: Omitting the `-s` option is something you'll rarely, if ever, want to do. A nonsymbolic link is a low-level Unix concept that entails creating a second "name" for a given inode on the disk. Remember that second column in the `ls -l` listing? Usually that shows 1, meaning a single "link" (filesystem directory entry) per inode (file). If it shows any number greater than that, it means an extra link has been created, and the filesystem can't distinguish any one link to an inode from any other link to that same inode. The symbolic link, by comparison, is just a pointer—an auxiliary entity that contains nothing but the path to the original item. Symlinks are much more common in Unix and much more likely to be what you need to use.

Find Files by Name or Contents

Mac OS X comes with a data indexing system designed to allow you to search quickly for any files in the entire system based on matching the search terms you type with either the files' names or their contents. This system, Spotlight, is built in to both the Finder (it's the oval Search bar in the upper right of every window) and the system's menu bar (the magnifying glass icon in the top right of the screen).

NOTE: Spotlight is similar in functionality to Google Desktop and to WinFS, the database-centric filesystem Microsoft hopes to ship in a future version of Windows. What these other indexing systems lack, though, is the Mac filesystem's Unique File ID, which allows Spotlight to keep track of files even if you move them from one folder to another. Because Windows lacks an equivalent of the Unique File ID, Google Desktop on Windows loses track of files if you move them.

A common task is to find a file whose name you know, or know in part. To leverage Spotlight for this task, you need to type only what you know of the file's name into the Search bar in a Finder window. As you type the file's name, all files whose names match what you've entered appear in the Finder window, sorted by file type (all images are bunched together, and all folders, music files, text documents, and so on). Select an item to see its path listed along the bottom of the window, from which you can open the item's enclosing folder by double-clicking it; or you can double-click any file to open it directly.

NOTE: Beginning with Mac OS X 10.5 (Leopard), a feature called Quick Look allows you to see a preview of any file for which a preview makes sense (such as PDFs, images, contacts, and so on) without opening the file's associated application. Quick Look previews are available by selecting one or more items in any Finder window, and clicking the "eye" icon in the toolbar (or pressing ⌘+Y).

You'll also notice that not only are files whose names match your search terms being found, so are files that happen to *contain* your search terms. Part of what makes Spotlight so cool is that every time a file is saved, Mac OS X indexes its contents into the Spotlight database, making it possible to search instantly for any occurrences of a text string in all files throughout the system. So if you remember even a tiny snippet of an iChat conversation you saved a few weeks ago, go ahead and type it in—Spotlight will find it. How cool is that?

You can also limit the searching scope by selecting from among the options in the bar along the top of the window: This Mac (your entire computer), the currently selected folder, the Shared folder, or any other folders you choose to add to the list of scopes. So if you're looking at your Pictures folder that's packed full of files, and you want to narrow down the list to just the ones whose names match a certain string, type that string and then click the **"Pictures"** scope to exclude files that aren't in that folder tree.

TIP: You can also perform Spotlight searches using the global search bar at the top right of the screen (click the magnifying-glass Spotlight icon to open it up). This kind of Spotlight search will find matches even in items that aren't strictly "files," such as email messages and Address Book contacts. Selecting these matches opens them in their respective applications, which illustrates that Spotlight is built in to all kinds of apps in the system, not just the Finder.

> **TIP:** Spotlight results have their own **File, View Options** panels, too, just like regular Finder views. Options you can select include grouping by date rather than by kind (files from Today are listed first, followed by Yesterday, Previous 7 Days, and so on), and sorting within a group by kind, date, or name.

Find Files by Kind, Date, or Other Attributes

```
File → Find
⌘+F
```

Spotlight's usefulness doesn't end there. Not only does Spotlight index all the textual contents of all your files, it also indexes attributes that vary depending on the file type. For example, remember all those extra file info fields you saw in the Get Info panel of a digital photo? You can use Spotlight to search on those too. I did a search for all my telephoto shots by looking for files with a focal length of greater than 49mm.

To accomplish this, you need to add criteria to any in-progress search by clicking the + button at the right side of the window, underneath the Search bar. Each time you click this button, it adds another attribute, which you can use to filter your search results or delete by clicking its – button.

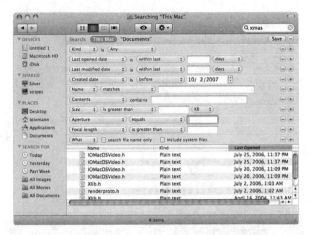

Figure 5.1   Just a few of the attributes you can use in specifying a Spotlight search.

The combinations of the Spotlight searches you can make are limitless (see Figure 5.1). You can, for instance, search for all the PDF files created in the past week, or the image files greater than 1MB in size, or all the Word files opened in the past two weeks that contain the word "obstreperous."

TIP: The Kind attribute submenu looks fairly limited, with only nine rather broad categories (such as Images, Movies, Presentations, and so on); but try selecting the **Other** option. This creates a text input box into which you can type specific file types such as "Microsoft Word Document" and "JPEG Image"; Spotlight's results appear in real time to match what you have typed so far.

Additional special attributes that are specific to certain file types, like the aforementioned focal length field, are available if you select the **Other** attribute type. You'll get a pull-out sheet with a long list of all the available attributes supported by any of the file types your installed applications report. This list can be very long, so it takes a moment or two to load. To speed up access to the attributes you'll be using frequently, you can enable the **In Menu** check box before you click **OK**, and the attribute you selected will be added to the list in the primary menu for each Spotlight criterion.

TIP: Choosing **File, Find** brings up a Finder window that's unlike others you might have seen: It's a ready-made Spotlight search window, with one initial attribute ready to be filled in (**Kind**), which you can use as-is, change, or further constrain by adding more criteria. It's what you'll want to use if you want to search for files based on criteria other than the name, because a regular Finder window won't give those criteria selectors to you until you start searching by name.

Save a File Search as a Smart Folder

File → New Smart Folder

Spotlight searches can get addictive; you might not be accustomed to having this level of visibility into your files' most intimate attributes, and you'll find yourself creating ever more elaborate searches to find files you never even realized you had. But each time you close a search window, all your carefully constructed search terms and criteria disappear. Isn't there a way to save them?

Of course there is: the **Save** button near the top right of any search window. This creates a Smart Folder, which is really a saved Spotlight database query. Anytime you open up a Smart Folder in the Finder, it performs the same query against your current set of files and presents the up-to-date list of everything that matches. This means that you can create a Smart Folder that shows you all the image files that you opened in the previous week—and it'll always show you the current last week's worth of images, no matter when you look at it. A Smart Folder's contents dynamically update to always stay in compliance with the search attributes you saved with it. I'm sure you're already thinking of a few clever uses you can put this feature to, right?

Smart Folders can be saved anywhere you like, although the default location—rather oddly—is a folder called Saved Searches that lives inside your Library folder. This is odd because you're not supposed to have to go into your Library folder in your normal daily computing. (You do, however, get the option to add freshly created Smart Folders to your Finder's Sidebar for easy access.) On the other hand, there probably isn't a better place for the Saved Searches folder to go. I recommend that you go ahead and create your Smart Folders there, and then make aliases to them that you can keep on your desktop or in another folder, or else put the Smart Folders into your Dock for one-click access.

NOTE: Smart Folders aren't "real" folders, and they don't behave quite like them in a variety of ways: right-clicking them in the Dock doesn't bring up a menu of their contents, navigating into them in Column view shows them as monolithic files that you have to

double-click to see into, and the Unix command line
has no idea what to make of them, other than to just
list them as opaque files.

There is, however, a third-party project afoot to rectify
this situation: SpotlightFS (http://code.google.com/p/
macfuse/wiki/MACFUSE_FS_SPOTLIGHTFS), a filesystem plug-in from the guys at Google who brought us
MacFUSE, a user-level filesystem plug-in architecture
for Mac OS X. With SpotlightFS installed, Smart
Folders attain all the transparency and flexibility of real
folders—even on the command line!

To uninstall MacFUSE:

http://code.google.com/p/macfuse/issues/detail?
id=36&can=2&q=

TIP: Spotlight contains some command-line functions,
too. The commands you'll be interested in are the
ones that begin with `md`, which stands for "metadata"
(the attributes used by Spotlight for indexing): `mdfind`,
`mdls`, and `mdutil`.Use `mdls` (as you would use `ls`) to
list files and their attributes, and then `mdfind` to construct Spotlight queries based on those attributes. You
can manipulate files' metadata using the `mdutil` command. See the `man` pages for these commands to learn
more.

Look Inside a Bundle

Show Package Contents

You learned about bundles and what they're commonly used for earlier in this chapter. Sooner or later, there
might come a time when you want to see what's in
a bundle; for instance, you might want to customize
the bitmaps that make up an application's skin, or you

might want to dig out the raw DV streams that make up an iMovie project. You can accomplish this using a command that's accessible only through the contextual, or right-click, menu of the Finder: **Show Package Contents**.

Find the item that you want to look inside, and then hold down Control while you click it (or right-click, if you've got a multibutton mouse). If it's not a bundle, the **Show Package Contents** option won't be there; but if it is a bundle, choose that option to open up a new Finder window whose navigation tree begins at the top level of the bundle and digs down from there.

You can delve into a bundle even more directly using the Unix command line. As you'll recall, the CLI doesn't know anything about bundles—to Unix, they look like regular folders. You can cd and ls your way into a .app, .rtfd, or .iMovieProj bundle just as you would any other folder, and any changes you make within the bundle will be invisible at the normal navigational layer of the Finder—you can swap out the skin bitmaps on your favorite applications, and your Mac will never be the wiser.

Take a Screenshot

⌘+Shift+3
⌘+Shift+4

Capturing images of what's on your desktop is one of those traditions of computing that's as popular as ever—and with good reason. Tech support and technical writing would be hamstrung without an efficient way to take screenshots. Fortunately, Mac OS X comes with a screenshot utility built right in, accessible through an undocumented keystroke: ⌘+Shift+4.

Pressing this three-key combination turns your mouse into a crosshair. Click and drag an area of the screen that you want to capture, and as soon as you release the button, the dragged area is captured into a file in PNG format called Picture 1, stored on the desktop. (Additional screenshots you take have their filenames incremented accordingly.)

Of more general use is the ⌘+Shift+3 keystroke, which captures the entire screen to a file. Also, you can have these built-in screen-capture functions copy the selected screen contents to the Clipboard, rather than to a file; to do this, hold down the Ctrl key at the same time (making the keystrokes ⌘+Ctrl+Shift+3 and ⌘+Ctrl+Shift+4, if your fingers are that nimble).

To capture a single window, or to capture a part of the screen after a time delay, you can use an additional obscure feature: press ⌘+Shift+4 as you normally would, wait for the crosshairs to appear, and then press the spacebar. This turns your cursor into a camera, which you can use to point at any open window— even windows that are partially obscured by others— and capture their contents at just the right moment with a single click.

Apple provides a rudimentary but useful tool called Grab, located in the `Applications/Utilities` folder. This application provides much of the same function- ality that's available in the built-in keystroke com- mands, plus a few additional options such as letting you customize the cursor. For most purposes, though, anything you can do in Grab can be done more easily and directly just using the built-in keystrokes.

TIP: If you want a really full-featured screen-capture utility, there's nothing better on the Mac than Snapz Pro X (http://www.ambrosiasw.com/utilities/snapzprox/). This $69 application takes advantage of the Quartz compositing layer to capture windows with drop-shadows intact against white backgrounds, making the Mac OS X borderless window style show up beautifully in documentation. It can also capture individual windows chosen visually, freely placed screen sections, or smoothly running movies with voice-over. It's a little bit expensive, but the Mac tech writer has no better friend!

Conclusion

There's clearly much more to the Finder than what's covered in this brief chapter; but most of it, frankly, you can probably figure out for yourself. The really interesting parts of what the Finder can do are in the rather more obscure and confusing features, such as Spotlight, and in how these features interact with other applications and with the Unix command line—not to mention how they could stand improvement. You've seen how the Finder's various views can be tweaked to your satisfaction, as well as how they've compromised their long-vaunted spatiality. You now know how Mac-style aliases differ from Unix-style symbolic links, and how to create both; you've seen how Spotlight can be used to create richly targeted searches, and how its interaction with the rest of Mac OS X and with the command line is limited in a few key ways.

This all just goes to show you that no matter how hard a company like Apple works to bring out a truly power-packed operating system, and no matter how well they succeed, there will always be room for improvement, and for tweaks that the adventurous— like you—can perform in pursuit of it.

6

Viewing and Editing Text Files

The Mac might be known for its aptitude with multimedia content—music, photos, movies, and all the rest of the stuff Apple builds its "digital hub" strategy on. But when it comes to squeezing the less well-known capabilities from your computer, particularly in the Unix layer, you'll find that plain text data is where all the action is.

Text documents come in two varieties: plain (also known as ASCII) and rich (which can take any of several specific formats, such as RTF, HTML, and Word). Rich text is styled, meaning that it can contain special formatting, such as fonts, bold and italic text, margins, centering and justification, variable line spacing, and much more—including embedded images and tables. Plain text contains nothing but the letters and numbers of the text itself: No formatting is allowed beyond what you can do with the spacebar and the Tab and Return keys.

Unix system functions are typically controlled through configuration files, which are written in plain text and designed to be editable using a command-line text editor. Similarly, most Mac applications are configured using .plist files, written in XML, that are similarly editable completely with nonspecialized text editor applications such as TextEdit. To really get the most out of your Mac, you'll need to know how to interact with text files both in the GUI and the Unix command-line environment.

NOTE: Many .plist files these days are saved in a binary format, which makes them faster for their apps to read them, but also makes them impossible for you to edit directly. The plutil command can be used to convert your .plist files between the binary and XML formats.

If you have the Xcode Development Tools installed (they're a free download from the Apple Developer Connection site, http://developer.apple.com/), the Property List Editor is a utility specially designed for editing .plist files, whether binary or XML.

Edit a Text File in TextEdit

Open
Open With

TextEdit is a bare-bones word processor, much like WordPad on Windows, whose primary purpose is to open and edit text documents. It can also be used for fairly sophisticated rich-text editing; this entire book, for example, is written in TextEdit. It will open and save most Word files, as well as HTML files that can be used in web browsers.

NOTE: Plain-text files that you edit in TextEdit stay in plain text. But if you create a new document in TextEdit and save it, it does so in RTF (Rich Text Format), which uses a markup language that makes it unsuitable for interoperability with the Unix command line. However, you can change a TextEdit document to plain text at any time, using the **Format, Make Plain Text** command.

If you need to edit a plain-text file that's used by command-line Unix utilities, TextEdit will do the job just fine; but it won't necessarily open in TextEdit directly if you just double-click it in the Finder. TextEdit expects the plain-text files you feed it to have .txt extensions; if they don't, as many Unix text files don't (remember, extensions mean nothing to Unix), you have to use a little bit of force and elbow grease.

config.txt   httpd.conf

Figure 6.1   A text file that opens natively in TextEdit, and one that doesn't.

Navigate to the file in the Finder and look at its icon. If it's a "text" icon, like the one on the left in Figure 6.1, you can double-click it to open it in TextEdit. If it's blank, like the one on the right, there is no default application set up to open the file, so you have to locate the TextEdit application in the Finder and drag the file to its icon to open it.

> **TIP:** Keep TextEdit in your Dock for easy access if
> you're going to be editing a lot of text files.

Another way to open any file in TextEdit—including
text files that have been set to open by default in other
apps, such as Word—is to right-click the file and
choose **Open With** from the contextual menu. If
TextEdit isn't one of the offered choices, you can
select **Other** and pick TextEdit from the file picker
that appears next.

Make whatever changes you want to in TextEdit, using
the mouse, the copy/paste functions, and all the other
benefits that any GUI application gives you. However,
be aware that if you try to apply any formatting—
bolding, italics, line spacing—to the file, TextEdit will
turn it into a rich-text document, and it won't save as
a plain-text file anymore, rendering it useless to any
Unix programs that rely on it.

> **TIP:** Typing special characters (such as accented vow-
> els) on the Mac is an endearingly quirky endeavor. The
> basic procedure is that you press Option along with a
> letter that represents a special combining character
> (such as E to create an acute accent), and then you
> press a second key for the letter that you want to com-
> bine with the previous accent or diacritic. For example,
> to create the é character, you'd type Option+E, then E.
> To make Û, it's Option+I, then Shift+U.
>
> Turn on the Keyboard Viewer palette to show what
> each key does when you combine it with Option.
> The Keyboard Viewer can be activated in the **Input
> Menu** section of the **International** pane of System
> Preferences.

Edit a Text File in Nano

```
nano
```

Sometimes TextEdit just isn't the right tool for the job. If you're already using the command line in Terminal, sometimes it's faster to use a plain-text command-line text editor to open a file, make some quick changes, and save it back out, than to navigate in the Finder all the way to where the file is and then go through the rigmarole of coaxing it to open in a GUI application.

Many Unix-heads will urge the use of the ancient and mysterious vi editor; but I prefer a more straight-forward one called Nano, and probably you will, too. The Nano editor is a GNU workalike and enhance-ment of the popular Pico written by the University of Washington, created to escape the licensing model and copying restrictions on Pico. In Mac OS X, the pico and nano commands both launch Nano.

```
Silver:/etc/httpd btiemann$ nano httpd.conf
```

Nano is operated entirely using keyboard commands, as befitting its nature as a command-line application. It will, however, expand to fill your entire Terminal win-dow, so if you're writing code or modifying long con-figuration lines, you can stretch your Terminal window to whatever size you want, and the editor will fill it.

NOTE: An apparent bug in Nano (in Mac OS X versions prior to Leopard) prevents it from resizing itself proper-ly if you stretch the Terminal window while Nano is run-ning; to avoid getting the display stuck, quit Nano (^X) and then resize the window before reopening the file.

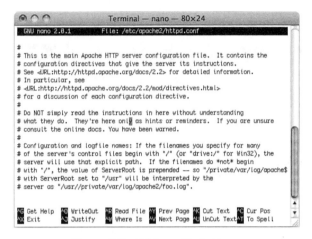

Figure 6.2   Editing a file in Nano.

You move throughout the document using the arrow keys, and type and backspace just as you would in any GUI program. (You'll have to get used to not being able to cut and paste using the mouse, though.) You can page up and down using the ^Y and ^V commands (that's Control+Y and Control+V), and move to the beginning and end of a line with ^A and ^E. You can even search for text using ^W, and spell check with ^T (although spell checking a Unix configuration file is bound to produce a lot of false positives). Cutting and pasting is done in whole lines—you can cut a line or a block of lines by pressing ^K; then press ^U to drop the cut lines in another location. When you're done modifying the file, press ^O to save it (specifying the filename when prompted—leave it the same to overwrite the original) and ^X to exit.

TIP: There's something cool you can do in Terminal to retain some of your mouse control: Hold down Option and click anywhere in a text editor window to move the cursor to wherever on the screen you want to be.

Display a Text File on the Command Line (Using cat)

cat

Sometimes you don't want to edit a file—you just want to see what's in it. For short files, the tool for this purpose is cat, the "catenate" program, which prints the contents of the file to the screen.

```
Silver:~/Desktop btiemann$ cat shoppinglist.txt
ground beef          3 lb.
frozen peas          1 lb.
broccoli             2 big crowns
milk                 1/2 gal.
dog food             86 cans
```

That's all there really is to cat—it prints the file and exits, so if the contents are longer than the height of your Terminal window, you'll have to scroll using the Mac OS X scrollbars rather than in any scrolling mechanism within the command line itself.

Viewing files that are longer than a screenful, in general, requires a somewhat more sophisticated program—a pager, which you'll learn about next.

NOTE: The cat program is actually useful for a good many other tasks—primarily as a component of other command-line incantations. Because the functionality of cat is so limited and yet so clear-cut, it's used for purposes such as feeding the contents of a file into another program (such as grep, the command-line search tool, which you'll learn about later in this chapter) or for adding the contents of one file onto the end of another through the use of data redirection operators (> and >>). These more advanced aspects of Unix are touched on later in this chapter (see "Send Filtered Output from a Command into Another Command or Text File").

TIP: Use the -n option on the command line to make cat print out line numbers next to each line in your text file.

Display a Text File Using a Pager (less)

As you might have gathered from the examples of Pico and Nano earlier in this chapter, Unix geeks love to play word games with the names of their programs. Nowhere in Unix is this more apparent than in the name of the now-standard pager, less, which was developed as a more feature-rich successor to the original pager, more. Yes, that's right: less has more features than more.

The more pager was originally named (as was its DOS counterpart) for its capability to display a text file one screenful at a time, printing "More" at the bottom to indicate that there was more text to follow, generally if you pressed the spacebar. Nowadays, pagers such as less (which is what you get if you type either the less or more command) not only scroll down page by page, but also line by line, and can move up, left, and right, too.

Open a file (or a list of files) in less like this:

```
Silver:/etc/httpd btiemann$ less httpd.conf
AddModule mod_auth.c
#AddModule mod_auth_anon.c
#AddModule mod_auth_dbm.c
#AddModule mod_digest.c
#AddModule mod_proxy.c
#AddModule mod_cern_meta.c
#AddModule mod_expires.c
#AddModule mod_headers.c
#AddModule mod_usertrack.c
AddModule mod_log_forensic.c
#AddModule mod_unique_id.c
AddModule mod_so.c
AddModule mod_setenvif.c
#AddModule mod_dav.c
#AddModule mod_ssl.c
#AddModule mod_perl.c
#AddModule mod_php4.c
AddModule mod_hfs_apple.c
AddModule mod_bonjour.c

#

:
```

As long as the colon prompt (:) at the bottom is present, there's more data to be seen if you press the spacebar (to move down one screenful) or use the arrow keys to move up or down line by line. Press the W key to move up a full screen. When you reach the end of the file, the colon prompt is replaced by (END), or if you're viewing more than one file at once, it moves on to the next file.

Quit out of the pager whenever you want by pressing Q.

Search for Text Within the Pager

```
less -I
```

That colon prompt at the bottom of the less pager isn't there just for decoration; it's also a command line of sorts for issuing directives within the pager environment, just as the regular Unix command line is a prompt for issuing commands to be executed by the shell. One of the typical commands you'll use within the pager is the slash (/) command, which in pager-ese means "search for the following text string," and is followed by the text you want to search for.

```
/Bonjour
```

Press the N key to find the next occurrence, or press Shift+N to find the preceding one.

You can search backward from your current position using the ? command:

```
?Bonjour
```

Remember, though, that searches are case sensitive—in other words, this search for Bonjour won't match occurrences of bonjour. You can launch less in a "not case-sensitive searches mode" by using the -i option on the command line, which matches all occurrences of your input string, as long as the input is all in lowercase, or the -I option, which matches all cases regardless of whether you put capital letters in your search string.

```
Silver:/etc/httpd btiemann$ less -I httpd.conf
```

TIP: The less pager has a lot more commands you can use, including many designed for programmers (such as the capability to pair up { and } brackets in blocks of code). Read about these in the man page: **man less**.

View the First Few Lines of a File

`head`

Sometimes you don't need to see the entire file— just the first few lines, either to make sure it's the file you're looking for, or (in the case of files that are automatically written out by programs, such as log files) to see what the first content written into the file was. The command for this lightweight, quick operation is head:

```
Silver:/etc btiemann$ head sshd_config
#       $OpenBSD: sshd_config,v 1.68 2003/12/29 16:

# This is the sshd server system-wide configuration
# sshd_config(5) for more information.

# This sshd was compiled with PATH=/usr/bin:/bin:/u

# The strategy used for options in the default sshd
```

```
# OpenSSH is to specify options with their default
# possible, but leave them commented.  Uncommented
```

As you can see, the default behavior of head is to print the first 10 lines. You can, naturally, adjust this number however you see fit. For example, to show the first 100 lines:

```
Silver:/etc btiemann$ head -100 sshd_config
```

View the Last Few Lines of a File

tail

If there's a whole command (called head) just for viewing the first 10 lines in a file, wouldn't you think there would be one to do the same for the last 10 lines? If there were, wouldn't you think it might be called tail?

Why, yes. Indeed you would.

```
Silver:/var/log/httpd btiemann$ tail access_log
127.0.0.1 - - [30/Jan/2007:20:42:19 -0800] "GET
➥/comics/today/overthehedge.gif HTTP/1.1" 20035882
127.0.0.1 - - [30/Jan/2007:20:42:19 -0800] "GET
➥/comics/today/calvinandhobbes.gif HTTP/1.1" 200
21418
127.0.0.1 - - [30/Jan/2007:20:42:19 -0800] "GET
➥/comics/today/pennyarcade.jpg HTTP/1.1" 200 89190
127.0.0.1 - - [30/Jan/2007:20:42:19 -0800] "GET
➥/comics/today/achewood.gif HTTP/1.1" 200 39859
127.0.0.1 - - [30/Jan/2007:20:42:19 -0800] "GET
➥/comics/today/megatokyo.gif HTTP/1.1" 200 300513
127.0.0.1 - - [30/Jan/2007:20:42:19 -0800] "GET
```

```
➥/comics/today/totq.jpg HTTP/1.1" 200 244664
127.0.0.1 - - [30/Jan/2007:20:42:19 -0800] "GET
➥/comics/today/www.the-whiteboard.com HTTP/1.1" 200
75552
127.0.0.1 - - [30/Jan/2007:20:42:19 -0800] "GET
➥/comics/today/sequentialart.jpg HTTP/1.1" 200
72815
127.0.0.1 - - [30/Jan/2007:20:42:19 -0800] "GET
➥/favicon.ico HTTP/1.1" 404 286
127.0.0.1 - - [30/Jan/2007:20:42:19 -0800] "GET
➥/comics/today/blanc.jpg HTTP/1.1" 200 72874
```

As you can deduce from this example, one of the primary uses for the tail command is to see what the most recent activity in an application is by looking at the last few lines of its log file. In this case, it's the web-sharing log, written out by the Apache server.

Just as with head, you can adjust how many lines you get to see at once:

```
Silver:/var/log/httpd btiemann$ tail -500 access_log
```

View the Tail of a File as It Is Continuously Updated

```
tail -F
```

If you're in charge of any services that run in the Unix environment on your Mac, such as a web or email server, or anything else that writes out a log of its actions, you might want to be able to keep watching that log as the application writes to it, so you know immediately when something happens without having to keep entering the tail command over and over.

Use the -F option to turn `tail` into a live view of your log file:

```
Silver:/var/log/httpd btiemann$ tail -f access_log
```

When you issue this command, tail does not exit, but instead keeps printing lines as fast as they are written into the file. On a busy web server, this can be overwhelmingly fast—intimidatingly so. Be prepared to be surprised at how many people are hitting your machine!

Press ^C to quit the `tail` program.

Seek for Patterns Within a Text File

`grep`

So you want to find a certain string of text wherever it occurs in the files in a certain directory? Forget Spotlight: It's overkill for that sort of thing. Spotlight is tailor-made for finding files of all kinds throughout the system and displaying them to you in pretty graphical previews, but it's of little help when you're dealing with the plain-text files in Unix, especially when you don't want the entire files—just the relevant contents.

Text files in Unix are defined not only on the basis of how many bytes they contain, but also in terms of how many lines they have. Lines are as much of a basic unit of division within a file as a single character is; in the plain-text world, operating on a line-by-line basis is efficient and direct, as you saw earlier in the discussion of the Nano editor and its line-by-line cutting and pasting.

With that in mind, it should stand to reason that
searching for text in a file or set of files doesn't return
mere names of matching files, but the lines within
those files that match your search text.

The command-line text searching tool in Unix is
called grep, and you use it like this:

```
Silver:/var/log/httpd btiemann$ grep "maakies"
access_log
127.0.0.1 - - [11/Jan/2007:01:04:05 -0800] "GET
➥/comics/today/maakies.jpg HTTP/1.1" 200 179574
127.0.0.1 - - [11/Jan/2007:01:04:13 -0800] "GET
➥/comics/2007.01.10/maakies.jpg HTTP/1.1" 200
179574
```

This grep command looks for the string maakies within the file access_log. The results of this command are
the complete lines that match the search string. If you
like, you can add the -n option, making grep print out
the line numbers as well:

```
Silver:/var/log/httpd btiemann$ grep -n "maakies"
access_log
14:127.0.0.1 - - [11/Jan/2007:01:04:05 -0800] "GET
➥/comics/today/maakies.jpg HTTP/1.1" 200 179574
61:127.0.0.1 - - [11/Jan/2007:01:04:13 -0800] "GET
➥/comics/2007.01.10/maakies.jpg HTTP/1.1" 200
179574
```

It gets better! If you don't know which files contain
the search string, you can use the wildcard operator
to search within all the files in the current directory:

```
Silver:~/Documents btiemann$ grep "milk" *
shoppinglist.txt:milk              1/2 gal.
```

This tells you the name of each file that matches, along with the matching line of text. If you're programming and you need to find every file that contains a certain function, this is the technique you'd use to find them.

NOTE: The grep command got its name from the semantics used in the prehistoric text editor ed, in which the command to search **g**lobally for a **r**egular **e**xpression and **p**rint the results was expressed in documentation as g/re/p.

Regular expressions (regexes or regexps) are an extremely powerful tool—arguably more so than anything else in Unix—and lie at the heart of grep-style searching. You can construct string-matching patterns of amazing complexity and flexibility using a few compact symbols. Read more about regexes at http://www.regular-expressions.info/.

Send Filtered Output from a Command into Another Command or Text File

What good is a list of the lines that match a certain string of text? Well, that's what's at the core of the Unix design philosophy: Using tools such as cat and grep and a few command-line operators to help direct the flow of data, you can orchestrate input and output through pipelines of commands, formatting and massaging your raw data into human-readable text. Now that you've seen how a few of those commands work, you can start putting them together.

Suppose, for example, that you're combing a web log file for an occasion where someone gained access to a certain unauthorized file. As part of your troubleshooting, you need to find not only the occasion where he accessed the file in question, but also the other files he viewed in the run-up to the incident. But the log file is several hundred megabytes in size, and every hit from the attacker's IP address is interspersed with hundreds of other hits from people all over the world. Where do you start?

One logical place would be to use grep to strip out all the lines that don't match the attacker's particular IP address:

```
Silver:/var/log/httpd btiemann$ grep "244.19.12.96"
access_log
```

Great, but this command spits out a few hundred lines—it seems that the attacker had been busy for days leading up to the incident, hitting your site on a regular basis. Well, that's not very helpful; it gets you closer to your goal, but thousands of lines are almost as unwieldy as millions, and just as difficult to find what you need in them. What next?

The answer is to start using pipes. The vertical bar (|) is an operator that lets you "pipe" the output of one command into another command. For example, here's how to take the filtered results and further filter them down to only a certain day:

```
Silver:/var/log/httpd btiemann$ grep "244.19.12.96"
➥access_log | grep "17/Mar/2007"
```

The lines that come out of this compound command are just the ones from that particular IP address *and* on that particular day. But suppose there are still too many of them to read comfortably. Well, why not use `less`?

```
Silver:/var/log/httpd btiemann$ grep "244.19.12.96"
➥access_log | grep "17/Mar/2007" | less
```

This command kicks you into the `less` pager, viewing the lines that came out of the previous two commands in sequence. You can now scroll through them at your ease.

Suppose you want to save the filtered results in a text file. For this purpose, you can use the redirection operators, > and >>. The > operator directs the output of a command into a new file; the > operator appends the data onto the end of an existing file:

```
Silver:/var/log/httpd btiemann$ grep "244.19.12.96"
➥access_log | grep "17/Mar/2007" > attack.log
```

Now you've got a file called `attack.log`, which you can peruse at your leisure to determine the attacker's movements. And if he comes back, you can do the same thing again, this time using > to send the new attack's information into the same file, tacked onto the end. Let's see Spotlight touch that kind of power!

Synthesize a Text File into Speech

Services → Speech → Start Speaking Text
say

The Mac has had text-to-speech synthesis since the very beginning. When the first 128K model was introduced onstage in 1984, Steve Jobs turned the stage

over to it to read a prepared statement to the crowd:
"Never trust a computer you can't lift!"

That same functionality is still in Mac OS X 23 years
later, and naturally it's been improved and enhanced
quite a bit. It's even available at the Unix command line.

Every application has a **Services** menu. This menu
contains operations that are available throughout the
system and that can be launched from any application,
using as input the content of that application. This feature is often used for sending chunks of text from one
app to another, such as creating a new Mail message
from a block of text you've got selected in TextEdit.
All you do is select the text you want to operate on
and then open the Services menu to find the service
and command you want to invoke.

This is how you can make your Mac speak the text
of any file you've got open in TextEdit, or in a web
browser, Mail, or even Terminal. First select the text
(press ⌘+A to select the entire file); then choose
Services, Speech, Start Speaking Text. The system
begins reading the selected text in the default system
voice. To stop it speaking, choose **Services, Speech,
Stop Speaking**.

TIP: Mac OS X comes with some 24 synthesized voic-
es, most of which are only of novelty value, but many
of which can do a pretty passable job of sounding natural. The new one in Leopard, called Alex, is the most
advanced Apple voice yet.

Choose a system voice in the **Speech** pane of System
Preferences.

The Unix command line has its own version of this
procedure: the say command. say can take a string of

text as input on the command line or a plain-text file as specified using the -f option:

```
Silver:~/Desktop btiemann$ say "I am Unix"
Silver:~/Desktop btiemann$ say -f War_and_Peace.txt
```

The say command does not exit until it's done speaking the text it's given, so pressing ^C will make it shut up.

The voice that say uses can be specified using the -v option:

```
Silver:~/Desktop btiemann$ say -v Alex -f
War_and_Peace.txt
```

You can even capture the spoken output as an AIFF audio file (which executes much faster than if the text were spoken in real-time):

```
Silver:~/Desktop btiemann$ say -v Alex -f War_and
➥Peace.txt -o War_and_Peace.aiff
```

Create a Compressed ZIP Archive of a File or Folder

```
File → Create Archive
zip
```

Mac OS X has Zip compression functionality built into the Finder, as well as into the Unix command line. This feature allows you to package up whole bunches of items into a single compressed file, which can then be sent through email, uploaded to the web for others to download, or archived to a disc for back-up purposes. Zip files can be unpacked by simply double-clicking them, restoring all their contents to their original hierarchies underneath a top-level folder with the same base filename as the Zip file they came from.

To archive files in the Finder, first select the item or items you want to package. Then, either in the **File** menu or in the contextual (right-click) menu, choose the **Create Archive** command. The wording of this command (and the name of the Zip file that results from the operation) depends on how many items you have selected. For example, if I'd selected only a single folder called Yosemite, the command would be **Create Archive of Yosemite**, and it would then create an archive file called Yosemite.zip. But if I'd selected three files, the command would be **Create Archive of 3 items**, and the resulting file would be called Archive.zip.

On the command line, the zip command (which corresponds to this Finder function) works a bit differently. You have to specify not only the names of the files to archive, but also the name of the resulting Zip file (being sure to add the .zip extension to ensure that the Finder and other computers can open it properly):

```
Silver:~/Desktop btiemann$ zip AlaskaTrip.zip
TripLog.txt Photo1.jpg Photo2.jpg
```

This command, however, is only for archiving the exact files specified on the command line and no others; if you give it the name of a folder, zip will archive the *folder*, but nothing inside it. You have to add the -r option to make it recurse into folders:

```
Silver:~/Desktop btiemann$ zip -r Alaska.zip Alaska/
```

This command creates the same kind of hierarchical archive that the Finder makes. Naturally, the reverse function is available:

```
Silver:~/Desktop btiemann$ unzip Alaska.zip
```

Conclusion

Text files are the heart and soul of Unix. The casual Mac user might be able to avoid working with plain-text files for an entire career, seeing only styled and rich text in GUI applications; but after you start poking around into the innards of the system and seeing how things are put together, you find yourself bumping into plain-text files more and more often, and needing better ways to take advantage of them than the basic tools the rich-text-oriented GUI gives you as an afterthought. This, more than any other reason, is why advanced Mac users end up making themselves more and more at home at the Unix shell within the Terminal. The text-manipulating tools in Unix are some of the most venerable and well developed in the world. As advanced operating systems get further and further from their plain-text roots, more people will necessarily keep rediscovering the solutions developed for Unix decades ago.

## 7

Ownership and Permissions

The history of Unix is a history of multiuser computing. Unix, from day one, was a "time-sharing" operating system, designed to allow multiple users to access the system simultaneously, run programs concurrently, and be safe from other users on the same computer prying into their data. Although earlier versions of Mac OS were single user (just as Windows was), as befitted the modest needs of desktop computing at the time, Mac OS X is a fully functional Unix and inherits the ownership and permissions system that made multiuser operation such an integral part of Unix in all its variations over the years.

Most Mac systems are used only by a single person, and so ownership and permissions seldom come into play. But if your Mac operates in a server role, or if you've got different user accounts set up for every person in your household, or even if you just like to tinker under the hood in areas outside your own Home folder, you'll need to know the intricacies of permissions and how to manipulate them.

NOTE: Refer back to "List Permissions, Ownership, and Other Details" in Chapter 4, "Basic Unix Commands," to refresh yourself as to how to view ownership and permissions in the command line, and see "Get Detailed File Info" in Chapter 5, "Using the Finder," on how to get the same information in the Mac OS X GUI.

Change the Owner of a File or Folder

chown

Changing the ownership of an item is seldom necessary during normal desktop operation of your Mac, but if you ever find yourself administering multiple users, the time will come when you have to tinker with who owns what. Someone might upload a file into your Drop Box folder, for example, and although it's in your Home folder tree, you might find that you can't modify it or throw it away because it's still owned by the user who uploaded it. Many other predicaments, equally implausible but also just as much of a pain to encounter, are possible.

Suppose I've got a file sitting in my Drop Box (a location in every user's Home folder structure where others can put files for your eyes only), that I can't seem to do anything with:

```
Silver:~/Public/Drop Box btiemann$ ls -l
➥Manuscript.doc
-rw-r--r--   1 frank   frank 150049 Jan  4  2007
➥Manuscript.doc
```

I can't change or get rid of this file because it's owned by the user frank, and the Unix permissions prevent anyone but the user from modifying it. To change the owner, I would use the chown (*ch*ange *own*er) command, giving it the Unix username of the user owner who should receive it (me):

```
Silver:~/Public/Drop Box btiemann$ chown btiemann
➥Manuscript.doc
chown: Manuscript.doc: Operation not permitted
```

Whoops! We don't have permission to make this change to the file. Well, that's exactly the problem we're trying to solve, isn't it? The answer, as you'll recall from Chapter 2, "Configuring Your Terminal," is to use the sudo command to execute the chown operation with elevated administrator powers:

```
Silver:~/Public/Drop Box btiemann$ sudo chown
➥btiemann Manuscript.doc
Password:
Silver:~/Public/Drop Box btiemann$ ls -l
➥Manuscript.doc
-rw-r--r--  1 btiemann frank 150049 Jan  4  2007
➥Manuscript.doc
```

Ah—much better! Now, as you can see, the file is owned by me, and because the permissions give the owner write capabilities (the first w bit is set), I can now modify this file as I see fit.

Change the Group Owner of a File or Folder

chgrp

You'll notice from the previous example that although the file's ownership was changed to me, the second ownership column in the detailed file listing—the group owner field—is still set to frank. The chown command operates only on the user owner of a file, not the group owner; this is part of the separation of permissions that allows members of a group to retain access to a file even if those members don't specifically own the file. But it can also cause problems if it's a file that you expect to have group access to, and yet it's owned by the wrong group.

The chgrp command works almost identically to chown; you give it the name of the group that should own the file, as well as the file's name, and stand back:

```
Silver:~/Public/Drop Box btiemann$ chgrp
➥btiemann Manuscript.doc
chown: Manuscript.doc: Operation not permitted
```

All right, fine—let's use sudo to authenticate as an administrator first:

```
Silver:~/Public/Drop Box btiemann$ sudo chgrp
➥btiemann Manuscript.doc
Password:
Silver:~/Public/Drop Box btiemann$ ls -l
➥Manuscript.doc
-rw-r--r--   1 btiemann btiemann 150049 Jan  4
➥2007 Manuscript.doc
```

There. Now, if the document were set so that the group owner could write to it (for example, if the second w bit were set), then not only would I be able to modify the file, someone else in the btiemann group would also have that capability.

But the second w bit is not set. How is that done? That's the job of the chmod command, which you'll see next.

TIP: `chgrp` exists as a standalone command for the sake of neatness; but you can also change groups using the `chown` command, by supplying both the username and group name at the same time, separated by a colon: `chown btiemann:btiemann Manuscript.doc`

NOTE: You might be accustomed to creating Unix groups by adding entries to the `/etc/group` file. This isn't the way it's done in Mac OS X. Rather, you use an entirely different mechanism called Directory Services, which can be accessed using certain command-line tools (such as `dseditgroup`) and the Directory Utility application (in your Utilities folder). Using Directory Services (which replaces NetInfo, the equivalent directory system that existed prior to Leopard) is not for the faint of heart and merits a whole book of its own. If you want to create Unix-style groups and perform other user-schema manipulations, I suggest picking up a book dedicated to Directory Services and advanced Mac OS X Server administration.

Change an Item's Permissions Symbolically

chmod

Ownership controls whose access rights the permissions bits map to. But the other side of the access control coin is the permissions bits themselves, which decide who gets to do what to each file.

As you'll recall, permissions are organized in three groups of three bits, each group corresponding to one of the three ownership classes: the owner, the group, and other users. Within each group are the read, write, and execute bits, which define, respectively, whether the file can be viewed, whether it can be modified or deleted, and whether it can be executed as a program. These nine bits, plus one more bit for special cases such as the sticky and setuid conditions, make up what's known as the file's *mode*.

NOTE: In Unix, an executable program is not defined by its extension (as with .exe in DOS/Windows), or even by its intrinsic properties as executable bytecode, but by the executable permissions bit. If it's set, you can execute the file as a program by typing its name (if it's in one of the common directories where system executables are typically found, like /bin or /usr/bin), or by typing its complete path and name (if it's not).

From this, it follows that the command to *ch*ange the *mode* is chmod. This command is quite versatile and can set a file's permissions either piecemeal or all at once, depending on how you specify the mode change argument. First let's look at how to change modes symbolically, using the same kind of letters that represent the permissions bits in an ls -l listing.

Recall that we've got a file with permissions set to "readable by all three classes, writable by owner only," which is expressed as -rw-r--r--:

```
Silver:~/Public/Drop Box btiemann$ ls -l
➥Manuscript.doc
-rw-r--r--   1 btiemann btiemann 150049 Jan  4
➥2007 Manuscript.doc
```

Suppose we want to make this file writable by the group as well, so that other users in the btiemann group can make changes to it. You'd use the chmod command as follows:

```
Silver:~/Public/Drop Box btiemann$ chmod g+w
➡Manuscript.doc
Now take a look at the permissions:
Silver:~/Public/Drop Box btiemann$ ls -l
➡Manuscript.doc
-rw-rw-r--  1 btiemann btiemann 150049 Jan  4
➡2007 Manuscript.doc
```

Aha—now that second w bit is set, meaning that the group has write access. The command used the argument g+w, which translates to "for the group, add the w bit."

Now suppose I change my mind and want to revoke not only the write permissions from the group, but also the read permissions from the group and others, making this a private file that only I can read:

```
Silver:~/Public/Drop Box btiemann$ chmod g-w
➡Manuscript.doc
Silver:~/Public/Drop Box btiemann$ chmod g-r
➡Manuscript.doc
Silver:~/Public/Drop Box btiemann$ chmod o-r
➡Manuscript.doc
Silver:~/Public/Drop Box btiemann$ ls -l
➡Manuscript.doc
-rw-------  1 btiemann btiemann 150049 Jan  4
➡2007 Manuscript.doc
```

There—now I'm the only one who can even view the file.

There's a quicker way to achieve this mode, though, and that's to set the permissions bits with an = sign, not a + or -, thus specifying what they should be exactly, not in terms of giving or taking away bits:

```
Silver:~/Public/Drop Box btiemann$ chmod go=
➥Manuscript.doc
```

This command sets the group and other users to no permissions at all by leaving off any value following the = sign.

Similarly, if you've just written a Perl script and you want to be able to run it from the command line, you need to set its executable for all three classes at once. Do that by leaving off the left-side letter altogether:

```
Silver:~/Desktop btiemann$ chmod +x test.pl
Silver:~/Desktop btiemann$ ls -l test.pl
-rwxr-xr-x   1 btiemann btiemann    9881 Feb   12
➥2007 test.pl
```

Now any user can read and execute the file, but only you can modify it.

And that's only half of chmod's capabilities.

Change an Item's Permissions Numerically

chmod

The symbolic notation for specifying a mode change is really convenient for those just learning how Unix permissions work or for quick one-time mode changes like adding executable bits or taking away write bits. After you've grown accustomed to how permissions work, though, you might find that a more direct way of specifying a complete mode all at once is called for.

To do this, you need to learn the numeric mode specification that the permissions bits symbolically describe.

A permissions string like `-rw-rw-r--` is actually stored as a string of actual binary bits that make up an octal (base 8) number with four digits: 0664 in this case. (For the purposes of this discussion, only the last three digits are really meaningful, so let's say it's 664.) Each digit represents one of the three ownership classes, and the pattern should jump right out: 6 means "read and write," and 4 means "read-only," apparently. To crack this code, you need to think of each digit as the sum of several unique binary numbers, as described in Table 7.1.

Table 7.1   **Numeric Representations of Permissions Bits**

Value	Bit	Meaning
0	–	No access
1	x	Execute
2	w	Write
4	r	Read

In base 8, a digit can have only eight potential values (0 through 7), and each value can be uniquely expressed as the sum of any combination of the values in Table 7.1, where each value can be used only once. For instance, a 6 is the sum of 4 and 2, a 3 is the sum of 2 and 1, and a 7 is the sum of 1, 2, and 4.

This means that if you have a permissions string with a 6 in it, you can read it as "4 and 2," or better yet, "read and write." A 3 is "write and execute." And a 7 is all three permissions at once. 0, naturally, means no permissions are granted to the ownership class in question.

So now you can read a permissions string of 664 as "user can read and write; group can read and write;

others can read only." What's more, you can define any permissions string in one fell swoop, using the appropriate numeric string.

To make a file private (read/write for the user owner, no permissions for anyone else):

```
Silver:~/Public/Drop Box btiemann$ chmod 600
➥Manuscript.doc
Silver:~/Public/Drop Box btiemann$ ls -l
➥Manuscript.doc
-rw-------   1 btiemann btiemann 150049 Jan   4
➥2007 Manuscript.doc
```

To make a file executable and readable by everybody—and writable by the user owner:

```
Silver:~/Desktop btiemann$ chmod 755 test.pl
Silver:~/Desktop btiemann$ ls -l test.pl
-rwxr-xr-x   1 btiemann btiemann   9881 Feb  12
➥2007 test.pl
```

I don't know about you, but the math geek in me thinks that's just plain cool.

NOTE: Just as with chown and chgrp, you'll be prevented from changing the mode on a file if you don't already have write access to it. Use the sudo command, as described previously, to authenticate as an admin and make the changes you need.

Change Ownership or Permissions Recursively

```
chown -R
chmod -R
```

The chown, chgrp, and chmod commands are designed to operate on individual files and directories specified on the command line, as you've seen in the preceding examples. You'll find that if you apply permissions changes to a folder, it changes the permissions only on the folder itself—not on any of its contents. This can be plenty annoying if you find yourself in possession of a whole folder tree of hundreds of files that you rescued from some hapless friend's ailing disk, and you can't modify any of them until you change the ownership and permissions on every single file in the hierarchy. Who has the patience for that?

Fortunately, the authors of the ownership and permissions manipulation commands recognized that need (possibly in advance, but more likely immediately after their first encounters with a huge hierarchy of someone else's files that they had to wrestle with) and built the -R (recursive) option into each command:

```
Silver:~/Desktop btiemann$ chown -R btiemann
➥Rescued\ Items
```

This command traverses the entirety of the folder hierarchy in the Rescued Items folder and changes each one's ownership to me. The chgrp and chmod commands support the same option, and it works the same way in each case.

TIP: If you want to see each file's name as it's modified, use the -v (verbose) option.

Change an Item's Ownership and Permissions Graphically

Now that you know how ownership and permissions are dealt with in the Unix world, it's time to see how it's done at the GUI level within Mac OS X. The most direct way to change the ownership on a file or folder is through the Get Info panel, which you learned about in Chapter 5. Select the item and then choose **File, Get Info**. At the bottom of the panel, expand the **Sharing & Permissions** section, which shows you the level of permissions you have for the file (such as Read & Write) and the ownership and access permissions for the three classes of users accessing the item: the owner, the group owner, and others.

Figure 7.1   Changing ownership and permissions in the Get Info panel.

For items that you own, all the fields are changeable, presented as drop-down lists containing only valid user and group names; and as soon as you change a setting it's immediately applied to the file as though you'd issued the corresponding chown or chmod command in the Terminal. For items that you don't own, the permissions fields are grayed out and can't be changed—but the ownership fields are changeable. As soon as you try to change the ownership on a file you don't own, Mac OS X presents you with an authentication challenge, which is the equivalent of the sudo command on the command line; if you can successfully enter your own password, and you're listed as an Admin user, it will proceed with the ownership change.

The GUI for ownership and permissions changes has an equivalent to the -R (recursive) option, too: the **Apply enclosed** button, which appears only when you're looking at the permissions of a folder. If you press this button, you're warned that it's a one-way operation that can't be undone, and then you're prompted for admin authorization, if necessary. This visual method is potentially easier to understand than the Unix method, although they are literally performing the same actions as far as the underlying Unix layer is concerned.

Graphically Configure Access Control Lists

The + and − buttons below the permissions table in the Get Info panel are for setting up Access Control Lists (ACLs), an increasingly popular and highly flexible method for enforcing permissions in the Unix world. With an ACL, the basic Unix permissions apply in the general case, but you can override those permissions for specific individual users or groups, in much the same way as a certain file type can be associated with a certain opener application, but individual files can be configured to open in a different application on a per-file basis.

Click the + button to create a new ACL entry for the item you're examining. This entry appears below the three standard Unix permission roles, and you can select the user to which it applies, along with the level of permission that that user should have. The ACL entry overrides any of the more general permission rules that appear above it in the table.

To remove an ACL entry, select it and click the – button. Note that the general Unix permissions rules cannot be removed.

Conclusion

Ownership and permissions, although key to a thorough understanding of Unix, don't come into contact with the average (or even advanced) Mac user's computing life all that often. The usage profile of a Mac is typically more application oriented than file oriented, and even an administrator will seldom have a need to manually adjust these intricacies of file management. Even so, on those rare but high-stress occasions such as the aforementioned theoretical disk recovery operation, or if you find yourself trying to install a piece of Unix software that requires you to tweak certain files' permissions (such as a web app that has to be able to write to files that aren't owned by the web server user), these techniques will serve you well, whether on your Mac or on any Unix-style system you might use.

## 8

Printing

Unlike most other aspects of Mac OS X, printing is one of those functions that's best dealt with on the graphical layer alone. There is theoretically a Unix interface to the Common Unix Printing System (CUPS) architecture that underlies Mac OS X's printing subsystem, but there's hardly anything it allows the casual user to do that isn't made apparent in the graphical layer, too—and usually in a more straightforward manner.

This isn't to suggest that printing is always easy, or that there aren't tricks to be learned, or things that can be done on the CLI level that are impossible in the GUI. As well as Mac OS X supports today's printer lineup, it's still one of the areas where the interface could stand some improvement. This chapter covers the basics of setting up a new local or network printer and then shows a few techniques for keeping your printing queue humming along smoothly.

Set Up a Local (USB) Printer

Most local desktop printers are designed to be compatible with Mac OS X right out of the box, and the operating system adds drivers for new models every time you upgrade to a new point release. The trick is in making sure the driver is present in the system even if you've bought a brand-new printer that was just released onto the market, and which might not have a driver in the OS yet. The first order of business, then, is to run Software Update and upgrade your system to the latest version if you're not already running it.

Next, you'll want to see if the system recognizes the printer as it should. Turn it on and plug it in using the USB cable. Then open up the System Preferences and go to the **Print & Fax** pane, and then click the **+** icon to add a new printer. This brings up the Printer Browser, a separate untitled window whose purpose is to allow you to configure new printers for your system. Make sure you're in the **Default** browsing mode, which lists all printers that can be discovered automatically.

If Mac OS X recognizes your printer, it should show up by model name in the list, and the Print Using menu should show a driver that's appropriate to your printer. If it doesn't, though—if you see only the **Select a driver to use** message—you need to install the driver from the disc that came with the printer. Close the Printer Browser window and follow the instructions in the printer's manual to get the driver installed. You might need to restart after installing the driver.

After you've installed the driver, go back into the Print & Fax Preferences and try adding the printer again, using the same procedure as before. This time it should be able to find and list the printer for you.

Fill in the **Name** and **Location** fields (these can contain any identifiers you want—they're to help you distinguish one printer from the next in your computer's list, and don't affect the printers' operation) and then click **Add**. The Print & Fax Preferences pane now shows your local printer as the default printer, and reports its status. If it says Idle, you're ready to go.

NOTE: The command-line equivalent of the Status readout in the Print & Fax Preferences is 1pq, which displays the printer queue's status and any pending entries. If it says that your printer is "ready," then all is well, and you can try printing a test document from any application.

Set Up a Network Printer

It's potentially less hassle to set up a network (IP) printer in Mac OS X than a local one, odd as that may seem. Network printers generally don't need to have local drivers installed, and (in the case of shared office or university lab printers) they're also seldom newer than the version of the operating system that you're running. This means you can probably find the printer model you're looking for in Mac OS X's printer list right off the bat; just make sure you know the printer name and model before you begin.

In the System Preferences, go to the Print & Fax pane; then click the **+** icon to add a new printer. This brings up the Printer Browser window, which allows you to specify the printer's network location and other information. Click the **IP** icon in the toolbar to set up an IP-based network printer.

The first three fields are where you configure the printer's location on the network. **LPD** is the default and generally most appropriate protocol to use, although **IPP** is also fairly widespread (check with your network administrator to see which protocol is right for your printer configuration). If the printer is a queue on a remote server, enter its IP address and queue name in the remaining two fields; otherwise, if you're going to be sending jobs to the printer directly, put the printer's IP address in the **Address** field and leave the **Queue** field blank.

The **Name** and **Location** fields are identifiers for labeling the printer in your own computer. Name is what will appear in your applications' Print menus, and the Location field is for helping you keep track of where each printer is. (Is Phoebus the one by the break room or the one next to the lab?)

The final field, **Print Using**, is where you specify the make and model of the printer. Pull down the menu and select the manufacturer to open the hidden menu of printer models for that manufacturer. (Some printers, such as those by Dell, are rebadged versions of printers by other manufacturers, such as Lexmark; see if you can find out what the original make and model is if you have a printer that isn't in the list.)

NOTE: If your printer or its manufacturer is not listed, ask your network administrator if there's a PPD file for your printer available. You can then browse for the file by selecting **Other** from the **Print Using** menu.

When you've found your printer's model, select it and then click **Add**. The printer is added to the list. You can now go ahead and try sending a test page from your favorite application.

TIP: If this is not the first printer you've set up, you can define which will be the default printer in all your applications by selecting it from the **Default Printer** menu.

Print Files in Any Application

File → Print
⌘+P

One of the hallmarks of the Mac is a consistency of design from one application to the next, particularly in how the menu commands are laid out. The Application menu (the one whose title is the app's name) always has the same basic components, such as an About command, the Preferences, the Services submenu, and so on. Similarly, every app's File menu has a few items that you can be sure to find. Among those is **Print**, whose universal keyboard shortcut is ⌘+P.

In the dialog sheet that appears when you issue the Print command, the default printer you specified in the Print & Fax preferences is preselected, and you can choose any other printer you've got configured. The Presets menu lets you define a custom paper-handling "recipe" using the third menu on the page, which presents a variety of options depending on which section is selected, from how many pages to print per sheet to how the printer should load its paper. These options are all up to you to explore.

What's interesting are the options at the bottom of the sheet, such as the **PDF** menu/button, which gives you many alternative options for capturing the print subsystem's output instead of sending it to the printer. Options in the PDF menu include saving what would have been printed as a PDF file (useful for archiving the receipts from web purchases, rather than sending them from your browser to an actual printer), a PostScript file, or a fax transmission to a destination you specify. You can even compress and encrypt your PDFs as you create them.

The Preview button takes the rendered output and sends it directly into the Preview application, your accustomed image-viewing program, but with the exception of a Print button at the bottom that lets you send the job straight to the printer after you're done previewing it.

TIP: Don't miss the annotation tools that Preview provides, including rectangular and oval callouts (the buttons in the toolbar at the top). This lets you add your own comments to a document right in the preview phase, before sending it on to the printer.

Print Files Using Drag-and-Drop

Printing from within an application is how you get the most control over your print job. But what if you have a text document that you want to send quickly to the printer without going through all that rigmarole of opening it in its native application, opening up the Print dialog, accepting all the default behaviors, previewing, and finally printing? Sometimes you just want to dash off a shopping list to the printer or make a quick copy of a PDF to grab on the way out the door. Mac OS X provides a way to do this, which is a little hard to find these days, but used to be called out as a major feature called Desktop Printing.

The idea is that you keep an icon of your printer sitting around in some convenient place—on your desktop, for example, or in your Dock—and then any file that you want to print, you simply drag to the printer icon, and it prints it immediately without asking for any further guidance or opening the file in its application. Sound like a good idea? I sure like the sound of it.

In the Finder, navigate into your Library folder (the one inside your Home folder) and then into the Printers folder. This folder contains icons for each printer that you've got configured in System Preferences. Each printer icon is really a mini-application that contains your personal settings for the printer and provides a shortcut to the printer's queue viewer (which you'll see more about shortly). It's a little bit hard to get to in that location, though, and so you'll need to put a shortcut to it in a more conspicuous place.

TIP: If you have the Print & Fax Preferences pane open and the printer list visible, you can just drag and drop entries from the list onto your desktop. This creates printer aliases in one fell swoop.

I like to drag the printer icon to my Dock, where items that need to be easily accessible can live comfortably. No matter what app I'm using, or even if my windows are all hidden using Exposé, I can grab a file off the desktop or out of a Finder window and drop it onto the printer in the Dock. Or, if you prefer, you can make an alias to the printer—select it and then choose **File, Make Alias**—and then put the alias on your desktop, wherever you want it, and with whatever name you deem appropriate.

Now printing is a simple drag-and-drop operation away!

Print from the Command Line

`lpr`

Because Mac OS X's printing subsystem is built on CUPS, the widespread open-source printing framework for Linux and other Unix-type systems, printing files from the command line is a pretty straightforward operation. If you've ever faced the pain of setting up a Linux or FreeBSD system for printing, wrestling with printcap files, and writing filter scripts, you'll love how ridiculously easy it all is when the hard work has been done by a company whose employees are paid to make it work.

The command to print a file is lpr. You use it quite simply:

```
Silver:~/Desktop btiemann$ lpr shoppinglist.txt
```

There's no equivalent of the printer options dialog here—CUPS sends the file straight to the printer, rather like using a drag-and-drop printer icon as in the preceding example.

Because the printing system is common to both the GUI and the CLI levels of the OS, you can print much more than just text files; lpr can print PDFs, images, and anything else you can print using the drag-and-drop method.

The lpr command has several options, which you can read about in its man page, but chief among them is -P, which lets you specify the printer—by name—you want to send the job to.

```
Silver:~/Desktop btiemann$ lpr -P Lab_LaserJet
➥resultdata.pdf
```

TIP: Some of these tips might seem to have pretty limited applicability to real life, but you'll find the darnedest situations come up where these kinds of techniques might be helpful. Suppose, for example, that you're in a lab on campus several buildings away from your room where your computer is, and you realize you need a document that's on the computer, but the printer's in the lab where you are. You can use SSH to log in to the Mac and then use lpr to send the print job to the lab (assuming, of course, that you'd set up the lab printer on your Mac previously). Just be sure to tell everybody what you're doing so you can bask in the accolades.

TIP: You'll see more about this later, in Chapter 14, "Sharing Files and Resources"; but the way to enable remote SSH logins on your Mac is in the Sharing pane of System Preferences (it's the **Remote Login** option).

List a Printer's Pending Jobs

`lpq`

Part of a good printing subsystem's job is to keep track of the printer's status and report to you what might be bogging it down, be it a queue of huge print jobs from other users or a technical fault such as a paper jam. On both the GUI and CLI levels, Mac OS X lets you keep an eye on your printer's queue of pending documents and its current status.

In the GUI, the quickest way to get access to a printer's queue viewer is by launching it from the drag-and-drop icon you learned how to create earlier in this chapter. (If you didn't create one then, now's a good time—and a good excuse—to do so.)

Another way to access the print queue is through the Print & Fax pane of System Preferences; select the printer you want to view and then click **Print Queue**.

In the graphical queue viewer, you can start and stop the print queue configured in the CUPS subsystem, pausing your pending jobs until the printer has worked through other people's jobs. You can also delete your pending jobs if you change your mind and don't want to print them after all.

At the command line, the equivalent is lpq, the command to invoke the line printer queue:

```
Silver:~/Desktop btiemann$ lpq
Lab_LaserJet is ready
Rank    Owner    Job  File(s)            Total Size
1st     btiemann  71  shoppinglist.txt   1024 bytes
2nd     frank     72  reservation.pdf    11982 bytes
```

This tells you the status of the printer (whether it's ready, printing, or stopped for one reason or another) and all the pending print jobs, including their sizes, owners, and queue IDs.

As with lpr, you can specify the -P option to view a different printer's queue. Another option you can use, if you really want to keep an eagle eye on things, is +*interval*, which lets you view the queue as a live-updating, autorefreshing list, rather like tail -f. The number you use in place of *interval* is the number of seconds between refreshes, which the system continues to use until the queue is empty.

Cancel a Print Job

`lprm`

We've all done it, and we all know the feeling: We've accidentally sent some massive job to the printer, some text document with hundreds of pages, or something sent through the wrong print driver so that each sheet of paper gets only a few bytes' worth of unprocessed PostScript code. No matter how much we press Escape, nothing stops the job, and we have to resign ourselves to the fate of the printer chewing uselessly through a whole stack of nice new paper. Sometimes all we can do is power-cycle the printer and reboot the computer to be sure the job won't get through. (Why can't these times be the ones where data stops getting through so darn reliably?)

Fortunately, when you're using a remote print queue, you've got a potential solution: you can delete a document from the queue before it gets sent to the printer, even while it's in the middle of printing. In the graphical print queue viewer, in which you've already seen how to list the pending jobs, click to select the job you want to get rid of, and then click Delete.

TIP: The **Stop Jobs** button isn't a secret utility to halt Steve Jobs's takeover of the computing world—sorry to disappoint you. You use this button to pause your computer's queue, which prevents your print jobs from being sent to the printer until you restart it by clicking **Start Jobs**. This can give you some much-needed time to collect your options.

On the command line, delete jobs from the queue using the `lprm` command. `lprm` takes a job ID, which you can harvest using `lpq`, as in the preceding example. For instance, to get rid of Frank's job, called `reservation.pdf`, enter the following:

```
Silver:~/Desktop btiemann$ lprm 72
```

If you have the GUI print queue viewer open while you issue this command, you'll see the job disappear from the queue after a few moments. It's nice when things work together, isn't it?

Once again, the -P option allows you to view a different printer's queue.

Troubleshoot a Problematic Print Job

The occasional print job will cause Mac OS X to choke. I've seen certain print jobs head merrily into the print queue, only for the printer's status to suddenly change to Jobs Stopped and its Dock icon to develop an exclamation-point marker. Restarting the queue seems to get it back to working order, but then printing the same job makes it come to a halt again.

What's going on there is that the CUPS daemon is crashing, generally because the data being fed to it is formatted in such a way that the driver can't handle it. Now, because data to be printed has to go through several transformations and encapsulations before it can be sent to the generalized output layer, you might be able to cause it to respond differently if you capture the print job as a PDF (as described earlier in this chapter) and then print the PDF. That might bypass whatever formatting error is tripping up the CUPS daemon.

TIP: The `lpstat` command gives you a command-line view into the print queue and its status, similar to what you see in the queue viewer in the GUI.

If that doesn't work, you can try looking in the CUPS logs for the details of the crash; these logs can be found in /var/log/cups, and you can view them using the `less` pager and other tools that you learned about in Chapter 6, "Viewing and Editing Text Files," or—if you prefer the GUI—you can use the application called Console (in your Utilities folder) that gathers together all the log files in the system, including the CUPS logs.

It's unlikely that you'll be able to deduce anything directly from the logs that will allow you to fix the problem, but it will give you details that you can submit to Apple or the CUPS development team in a bug report from the field. It could be that your particular combination of data format, printer model, and operating system triggers an elusive bug in the CUPS daemon; and if you're able to contribute your experience and data to the global open-source effort to improve projects like CUPS, you'll gain many geek points. And isn't that more important than printing some silly document, in the long run?

TIP: CUPS even has a web interface, which you can access using a regular browser as long as it's on your own machine. The URL is http://localhost:631/.
This interface gives you useful views into the print queue's status, lets you view previously completed jobs, and many other administrative tasks that are impossible in either the command line or the Mac OS X GUI. You'll have to enter your user account name and

password to gain access to the Web interface, and it is not accessible from another machine.

Conclusion

Printing is one of those unglamorous, infrastructural areas of computing that you never really think about until it doesn't work anymore. Even so, it's important to be able to make even the less-sexy parts of your operating system sing and dance, particularly when it can make your life significantly easier to have a few shortcuts in place. Mac OS X has done a pretty good job of presenting a coherent graphical interface to your printer queues and a *really* good job of integrating the esoteric details of Unix printing into an OS that combines a GUI and a Unix CLI, with both sides equally able to interact with your modern printers. All it takes is a little familiarity with what you're doing to really be able to take advantage of it.

To learn more about the CUPS system and what command-line tools are available for it, refer to its website at http://cups.org.

## 9

Working with Applications

Even an operating system with as many bells, whistles, and toys as Mac OS X is little more than a curiosity without applications. It's in the applications, whether produced by Apple or by third parties, where all the real work gets done.

Every application has its tips and tricks for experts, but to talk about them all would take a bookstore rather than a book. Still, there are quite a few functions that are part of the operating system and apply equally well to any and all applications you might run. This chapter talks about a few of these features and techniques that allow you to focus your time and attention most effectively on your work.

Install an Application

On the Mac, an application is not the widely scattered, loosely associated collection of binaries, data files, documentation, libraries, and Registry entries that an app on Windows typically is. Instead, as you saw in Chapter 5, "Using the Finder," Mac apps are bundles—each one a single icon that you can move and copy anywhere in your system just like any other file. What's more, you can launch an application no matter where it is: in your Applications folder, on your desktop, somewhere else in your Home folder, on a remote network volume, in a disk image, or on a CD. Because each application bundle contains all the stuff the program needs to run, it doesn't matter where it's installed.

TIP: Because the Mac doesn't care where an app is located on the disk, and because application icons are well behaved, discrete items rather than folders full of unstructured files like on Windows, Mac OS X needs no equivalent to the Windows Start menu, which is a front-end to the Program Files folder and the executable files within its subfolders.

Rather, the Applications folder itself is a Start menu of sorts, and you can make it even more like one by adding your Applications folder to your Dock. Right-click it to pop up a launchable list of all your applications that you keep in that folder (which you should, for the sake of good form and neatness).

This behavior also means that installing an app on the Mac is a matter of dragging and dropping. When you download an app from the Web, it usually comes in the form of a *disk image*, which you'll learn more about in Chapter 10, "Working with Disks." (Disk images, which usually have the extension .dmg or .img, are frequently used for Internet software distribution because they are easily burned to actual CDs or DVDs for archives and for installation on multiple computers.) When you mount the downloaded disk image, its top-level window appears in the Finder just like any other mounted disk, and this window usually contains not only the application icon itself (which you can launch from right there in the window if you want to try it before installing), but also instructions on how to install the application. More often than not, these instructions amount to nothing more than "Drag this application icon to your Applications folder." Open a second Finder window for Applications, or aim your mouse at the Applications folder icon in your Dock or Finder sidebar, and drag the app there to copy and install it. That's all there is to it!

NOTE: When you drag an icon from one Finder window to another, it generally moves the item; but if you're dragging from one volume to another, Mac OS X duplicates the item instead. (You can see by the green + icon next to the mouse pointer what it's going to do.) Holding down the Option key switches the operation from move to duplicate, or vice versa, depending on where you're dragging the item.

Dragging and dropping doesn't always work, however. If you insert an installation CD or mount a downloaded disk image and are confronted not with a launchable application icon and drag-and-drop installation instructions, but with a "package" file (with an extension like .pkg) or an "installer" icon, you need to double-click that file to run an installation program.

This method is usually reserved for large apps such as iTunes or Microsoft Office, which must run scripts at installation time for ensuring the integrity of your data, upgrading your preferences, or installing files outside the location where you put the actual app. (iTunes, for example, installs not just the player application but also a "helper app" that watches for connected iPods and handles Internet lookups for track names on inserted CDs.) Because any operation that alters files in privileged locations (such as Applications) requires administrative credentials, you are prompted to enter your name and password to proceed.

After that's done, you can launch the app from the Applications folder with a double-click.

Deinstall an Application

The relative simplicity of app installation on Mac OS X really pays off in the deinstallation of apps you don't want anymore. Whereas on Windows, getting rid of a particularly ill-behaved program involves not only deleting all the related items in Program Files, but also running deinstallation scripts and sometimes manually cleaning out the Registry to get rid of orphaned keys that might cause problems later, on Mac OS X—which has no Registry—it's literally as simple a matter as throwing the application icon in the Trash. That's it.

Oh, sure, you might be bugged by the user-specific preferences file still sitting around in your Library/ Preferences folder; but without the application to apply it to, Mac OS X won't do a thing with that file, and it won't harm or hinder anything else on the system. Feel free to get rid of it if you want (it's usually labeled with a name matching the application's name, or with a reverse domain string such as com.ksuther.chax.plist), but it's not important unless you're trying to clean all your identifiable data off your disk.

The exception to this state of affairs is in the afore-mentioned applications that require installation programs, such as iTunes, Word, and so on. Chances are good that these apps install more on your disk than just preferences files in your personal Library folder. They might install frameworks, helper apps, kernel extensions, or other extraneous pieces in your system-level Library folder, and you won't know where or which files were added. In these cases, it's still usually less problematic than rogue Registry entries, but it's no good to have system-behavior-altering additions floating around. Unfortunately, there's no universal way to find and delete these items. The best you can hope for is that an app that comes with an installer program also comes with an uninstaller program (and that it works as advertised).

Find Common Application Functions

One of the hallmarks of the Mac is that, because all applications are developed using the same toolkits and by developers who tend to value consistency, every application uses the same basic menu commands and metaphors. There's no mystery in a Mac app when you're trying to figure out where the Preferences are—is it in Tools? Options? Edit? Are they called Preferences, or Options, or Settings? Nope—on the Mac, it's always Preferences, and it's always in the same place.

Here is a list of some of the most common menu commands that can be found in nearly every Mac app, as well as the standardized keyboard shortcuts to execute them.

Table 9.1   Common Standard Menu Commands in Applications

Command	Menu	Keyboard Shortcut
About Application	Application	
Preferences	Application	⌘+;

Table 9.1   **Continued**

Command	Menu	Keyboard Shortcut
Save	File	⌘+S
Save As . . .	File	Shift+⌘+S
Print	File	⌘+P
Close Window	File	⌘+W
Cut	Edit	⌘+X
Copy	Edit	⌘+C
Paste	Edit	⌘+V
Help	Help	⌘+?
Switch Windows		⌘+`
Switch Applications		⌘+Tab
Hide Application	Application	⌘+H
Quit	Application	⌘+Q

This list is by no means exhaustive, and you can familiarize yourself with the rest of the most common menu commands just by poking around. These, though, are the ones most likely to affect you in your daily computing.

TIP: Try holding down Option while a menu is open. Some of the menu commands will change to "alternative" versions, such as **Quit** turning into **Force Quit**.

TIP: Mac OS X lets you redefine the keyboard shortcuts for a lot of commands and add new ones for additional commands that don't already have them. In System Preferences, go to the **Keyboard and Mouse** pane, and then the **Keyboard Shortcuts** section. Click the **+** button, select the application, and enter the command name in the **Menu Title** field. This field's label is misleading: what you need to enter is the name of the command as it appears in the menu. For instance, to create a shortcut for **Edit, Prevent Editing**, you would enter **Prevent Editing**.

The modifier keys on the Mac's keyboard are not labeled with the symbols used in the menus, at least on the U.S. keyboard layout. Table 9.2 gives the keys' names, symbols, and what they're generally used for:

Table 9.2   **Modifier Keys on the Mac**

Symbol	Name	Function
⌘	Command	Combines with letter/number keys to create command shortcuts.
⌥	Option	Creates "alternative" versions of commands and characters.
⌃	Control	Primarily used for compatibility, as in Terminal CLI.
⇧	Shift	Creates capital letters and nonalphanumeric symbols, as well as secondary commands with ⌘.

Change a File's Default Opener Application

Open With

As you learned in Chapter 5, the Get Info panel can be used in the Finder to determine what application a file will open in when you double-click its icon, based on the default application that Mac OS X associates with a given file extension. You can also use it to override the systemwide setting on a per-file basis, telling the system, for example, that although you want most JPEG files to open in Preview, you want this *particular* JPEG file to open in Photoshop.

Open the **Open With** section of the Get Info window for a given file. In the menu beneath the heading is listed the default opener application for that file's type. Open the menu to see a list of all the applications that advertise themselves as being able to open files of that type, with the systemwide default marked as **(default)**.

Change the menu selection to the app you want to use instead of the default one. This setting is immediately applied, and the file's icon changes to one more appropriate for the selected app. From now on, double-clicking the file opens it in the new app, whereas all other files of that type still open in the default app.

You can change the default application for the selected file's type (and extension) by clicking the **Change All** button. If you do this, all files of that type will change to the new app's icon style.

Quit Applications to Conserve Memory

⌘+Q

If you're accustomed to Windows, you might be caught off guard by the Mac's *modal* style of windowing, in which the frontmost application takes over the entire desktop context and the menu bar at the top of the screen, even if it has no windows open. This can lead many an unwary user into thinking that he has quit an application, just because all of its windows are closed. Yet, unless you actually select the **Quit** command from the Application menu, the app continues running and consuming memory. This isn't as much of a problem in the modern age as it was in years past—with Mac OS X's robust virtual memory system, an app that isn't being used simply gets paged to unused space on the disk—but some apps might continue to chew up processor time in the background, even if no windows are open.

It's best to get in the habit of quitting applications using either the explicit **Quit** command in the Application menu or the ⌘+**Q** keyboard shortcut, rather than just clicking the red **Close** button in the top-left corner of the window you're working in. That button closes the window, to be sure, but it doesn't necessarily quit the application. This behavior is contrary to that of Windows, in which the application context is usually synonymous with the window context (except in the case of some metaphor-busting apps such as Web browsers).

NOTE: Some applications, just to be contrary, *do* quit when you click the **Close** button in the window title bar. These apps are most frequently utilities, such as you'd find in the Utilities folder; but also some headliner apps, such as iMovie and the other iLife and iWork apps, have a similar behavior, returning you to a "launch" screen that lets you begin a new project, open an existing one, or quit. These are apps that are designed to use only a single window for their operations, and a second cannot be meaningfully opened—thus, closing the only window is seen as synonymous with quitting the app session.

Also, while you're working, get in the habit of checking your Dock to see if any apps are still running that you don't need sitting around anymore. Running apps are denoted by a little blue light under their icons. If you see one, right-click or Control+click its Dock icon and choose Quit from the pop-up menu.

TIP: Of course, if you prefer, you *could* just keep the app running at all times—sometimes, especially if the app is a large one that takes a long time to launch, it's worth having it sitting around running and unused if it saves you the time of having to launch it from scratch every time you need it.

Force Quit Misbehaving Applications

```
Force Quit
kill -9
```

No application is perfect. Sometimes an app might get stuck or hang, and it no longer responds to your mouse or keyboard input, even though it might still be consuming so many resources that it drags your system to a standstill.

Mac OS X provides a couple of ways to recover from this kind of situation. The first is to use the **Force Quit** command, which is found in the Apple menu. Choosing this menu command (which should be available from within any app—if your menus are frozen, try switching to the Finder by clicking in an empty part of the desktop) brings up a floating window with a list of all the running applications and a Force Quit button. Select the misbehaving application and click the button to kill it forthwith.

Alternatively, use the ⌘+**Option+Esc** key combination to summon the Force Quit window without using your mouse and navigating the menus.

TIP: Another way to target an app for termination with extreme prejudice is to right-click or Control+click its icon in the Dock while holding down the Option key. Choose the Force Quit option from the pop-up menu that appears.

There are, however, some times when you need to kill a running program that isn't visible to the Finder or the Force Quit window. Mac OS X runs many processes in the background all the time, not all of which are graphical applications with menus and windows and the like. Some such processes are mds and mdimport (daemons that handle indexing data for Spotlight), DashboardClient (one instance of which runs for every Dashboard widget you launch), dotmacsyncclient (which handles synchronizing your data with the .Mac service), iTunesHelper (which watches for inserted CDs and looks up their track names online), and many others that are part of the Unix subsystem. Any of these programs can go haywire just like a graphical user app can, and you might need to kill it to get your system back. You just can't use Force Quit to do it.

Instead, you can use the Terminal and the Unix CLI. First, use the ps command (like ls for "list," only for processes) to find out the process ID of the misbehaving program:

```
Silver:~ btiemann$ ps -wwwax | grep iTunes
234  ??  S      0:00.27 /Applications/iTunes.app
```

```
➥/Contents/Resources/iTunesHelper.app/Contents/
MacOS
➥/iTunesHelper -psn_0_2097153
861   ??  S     42:23.03 /Applications/iTunes.app
➥/Contents/MacOS/iTunes -psn_0_15859713
 2488  p1  R+     0:00.00 grep iTunes
```

(The -a option shows all users' processes, not just your
own; -x shows all processes regardless of whether they
were launched from a terminal; and the three -w
options make the output lines as long as possible so
that you can read the entire command strings and tell
which one you're looking for. This also makes it easy
for you to filter the output using grep to find processes
matching a certain string, as you saw in Chapter 6,
"Viewing and Editing Text Files.")

It seems that our troublemaking iTunesHelper application has the process ID 234. We can now use the kill
command to destroy it. The kill command is actually
more aggressively named than it needs to be; its real
purpose is to send execution-control signals to running
processes, which can be anything from "quit gracefully"
to "shut down and restart yourself," depending on the
numeric signal you pass with it. In this case, however,
the signal we'll be sending is -9, the KILL signal, which
really does mean as much business as it sounds:

```
Silver:~ btiemann$ kill -9 234
```

That should immediately end the process. If it's a critical system process with what's known as a "watchdog"
watching over it, such as the Dock process or the
WindowServer daemon, the system will immediately
relaunch the process; but this time it should do so
cleanly and without spinning out of control again.

Restore an Application to Its Default Settings

Library → Preferences

That favorite app that you use every day—it worked fine just yesterday. Yet now it's crashing. What gives?

Or suppose that you were fiddling around in some app's Preferences, and now it's in some state or mode that you don't like—but you can't figure out how you got it that way or how to undo it. You liked it fine when it was in its default configuration right out of the box. What do you do?

Here's where the Mac's lack of a Registry really comes in handy. Rather than storing your preferences for each individual third-party application in a central Registry, or in disparate configuration files all over the disk, each application keeps a "preference file" in your Preferences folder, which lives inside Library, under your Home folder. The settings contained in a preference file are localized to your user environment and don't apply to any other user on your computer. What's more, if you throw the file away, the application just starts over from scratch and creates a new one. That's how you restore a Mac app to its factory default settings: what's popularly known as "trashing the Preferences."

TIP: Quit the application in question before you trash its preference file. If you don't, the app might write out its running configuration to a new preference file at the time you quit it, overwriting any work you did with the same old preferences you were trying to get rid of.

As you saw earlier in this chapter, preference files are usually named in such a way that you can identify what application they go to. Some are naturally named files, such as `DivX Decoder 5.1 Preferences`; others use a reverse hierarchical dotted domain naming scheme that mirrors the domain of the company that wrote the software, such as `com.apple.TextEdit.plist`. Some companies even create whole subfolders for their apps' preferences, such as `Microsoft` and `ICQ`. It'll generally be pretty easy to figure out which file goes to the app you're concerned about; if you have any trouble, just put the app's name in the search bar in the top right of the Finder window and limit the search scope to "Preferences" using the buttons under the toolbar.

You can throw the preference file away immediately, if you're sure it's what you need to do; or, if you're just trying to track down a specific problem but don't want to lose all your saved settings, try moving the file to a neutral location, such as your desktop. Then relaunch the application. It should be restored to its original, working state. Then you can build your settings back up, one by one, until you discover what you did that made it start acting funny in the first place.

Find Application Windows with Exposé

```
All Windows (F9)
Application Windows (F10)
Desktop (F11)
```

One of the crowning features of Mac OS X 10.3 (Panther) was its solution to the age-old problem of application switching in a multiwindowing environment. In the old days, you had to switch from app to

app, sight unseen, using nondescriptive buttons in a
taskbar or opaque application icons in a Dock, or (in
Windows in particular) you had to use keystrokes to
tab between open app windows with seemingly identical thumbnail icons that told you nothing about what
each window looked like. Shuffling windows around
was a tedious business until the arrival of Exposé,
which takes advantage of Mac OS X's Quartz compositing layer to scale each window so that every single open window in your system can be tiled on the
same screen, with their contents updating live, and you
can select the one you want with a glance and a click.
Even Windows Vista's Flip 3D feature, which aims to
solve the same problem, is arguably not as elegant a
solution—more flashy, certainly, but lacking the simplicity of tiled 2D windows in which you can see all
of every window's contents, as well as its complete shape
and relative size, and pick any one regardless of its position on the screen or whether it's "in front of" the rest.

The concept is simple: Press **F9**, and all the windows
in all your open apps are tiled across the screen. Click
the one you want, and it springs to the front. To tile
only the windows in your current application (such as
all the images you're currently working on in
Photoshop), use **F10**.

The third Exposé method, desktop (**F11**), is my
favorite: It makes all the open windows scoot off the
edges of the screen, giving you interactive access to
whatever's on your desktop. It's like the analogous
Taskbar button in Windows, except that it always
remembers which windows are where on the screen,
and it doesn't interfere with your choices to minimize
or hide certain apps. Pressing F11 again always brings
your windows back the way they were before you
started.

Start using this technique and you'll find that all sorts of time-saving workflows are now open to you. I might want to attach a file that's sitting on my desktop to an email message I'm writing. I can press F11 to dismiss all the windows, click and hold on the file on the desktop, press F11 again to summon all my windows back again, and drop the file into the message. It's as though I'd positioned the icon in a visible part of the desktop to begin with, except I no longer have to think in advance like that. I can also drag items from one application to another, such as by selecting and dragging some text in a web browser, pressing F9 to tile all open windows, hovering over my TextEdit window until it pops to the front, and dropping the copied text into it.

TIP: You can change the Exposé key commands in the Exposé & Spaces pane of System Preferences, if the defaults aren't convenient for you. You can also set them to be triggered by moving the mouse into any of the four corners of the screen or by clicking any of the auxiliary buttons on your multibutton mouse. There's nothing quite like being able to squeeze the sides of your mouse and have all your windows whoosh off to the sides when your boss walks by.

Expand Desktop Real Estate with Spaces

F8

Even with Exposé, sometimes there's just not enough space for all your apps to live comfortably. Unix and Linux users have for years enjoyed a feature not available on the Windows or Mac desktop without add-on software: virtual desktops. This feature gives you not just one, but many desktop windows to put applications in, almost like having multiple monitors hooked up. A click or a function key could take you from one virtual screen to the next; all your icons and toolbars would still be there, but the applications that are shown are specific to the virtual screen you're looking at. Conceptually it's just another way of minimizing or hiding apps—you put them on a different screen, and then you switch screens to find your other apps, rather than switching app windows.

Mac OS X Leopard brings virtual desktops to the Mac with Spaces. Taking advantage of the scaling and compositing engine used in Exposé, Spaces not only lets you switch between virtual desktops like in any traditional Unix window manager, it also lets you scale the entire workspace onto your single screen (by pressing F8) so you can see at a glance which apps are where. You can even drag apps from one virtual desktop to another, arranging things just the way you like them. The traditional number of virtual desktops is four, but you can create as many as you need to hold all your stuff.

Automate a Workflow

Automator

Sometimes you might find yourself doing the same set of menial tasks over and over, such as scaling a bunch of image files or changing a set of filenames to add tags or labels. Every power user has her own recurring workflows, depending on her work or how she likes to run her computer; users are so different in their individual computing needs that nobody ever writes applications to handle these little tasks we need to accomplish every day, and not everyone is a programmer able to write such apps on their own.

That's what Automator is for. This utility, included with Mac OS X and available in the Applications folder, lets you string together data and assets from one application, send them through another, and take that app's output and feed it into yet another, performing scripted actions every step of the way. If this sounds familiar, it's because it's like a graphical version of the pipes and data redirection that you saw in Chapter 6, where you learned how to string together a series of Unix commands to filter and slice up the data into a manageable form. Automator brings that concept to the level of the mere mortal and works with more kinds of data than plain text.

All your installed apps are listed in Automator's left pane; you can click one to see all the actions you can address, such as telling the Finder to prompt you for a list of files or to create a new folder, or telling Safari to connect to a certain website. Drag these actions into the right pane to create a workflow, with the output of one action feeding into the input of the next, and each action's options tuned to your needs. Keep adding actions to the chain until you've created a workflow that you can save in its native format so that it operates from within Automator or as an application that you can launch independently.

Automator is a full-fledged application, with enough functionality to warrant a whole book on its own. If you're the kind of user who has a need for what Automator can do, you'll pick it up in no time.

Schedule a Recurring Command

```
cron
crontab -e
```

Being a server-class operating system, Unix has always had a need for the capability to schedule certain tasks—file cleanups, mail delivery, news synchronization, security audits—to run automatically on a recurring basis. This task has been performed for many years now by the cron daemon, a utility that runs as a background process and reads users' scheduling files called *crontabs*, executing the commands in them at the times specified.

To set up your own crontab file, you need to use the Unix command line and the crontab -e (edit) command.

TIP: If you want to avoid the command line, you can use a simple GUI frontend to your crontab file, such as Crontooie (http://quicksilver.caup.washington.edu/software/Crontooie/).

```
Silver:~ btiemann$ crontab -e
0 * * * * /Library/WebServer/Documents/comics/
➥get-comics
~
~
"/tmp/crontab.y2eE9hF4eD" 2L, 58C
```

What you see here is the strange and ancient vi editor, whose interface is more similar to the less pager than to a text editor such as Nano. Don't worry—you need to know only a few simple commands here. First, press the I key to enter Insert mode. Now you're ready to type.

The `crontab` table consists of as many lines as there are scheduled items, and each line is broken into six fields, separated by spaces or tabs. The first five fields have the following meanings: minute, hour, day of month, month, and day of week. The sixth field is the command to be run.

Each of the first five fields can be either a number (specifying a time or date) or an asterisk (meaning that the field doesn't restrict whether the action takes place). For instance, to execute a command at 3:00 in the morning on every Monday, you would enter the string: `0 3 * * 1` (the minute is 0, the hour is 3, the day and month aren't important, and the weekday—where 0 or 7 is Sunday—is 1, or Monday).

The sixth field contains the command you want to be run, using your user permissions. If this command has spaces in it, enclose the entire command in quotes.

When you're done, press Esc to exit Insert mode; next, type `:w` and press Return to save the file. Then type `:q` and press Return to exit. This saves your new `crontab` file, and Mac OS X will execute your command at the time you specified, recurring however often you requested.

TIP: There are several other syntax possibilities for the `crontab` file, which allow you to specify events that should occur at a list of disparate times or dates, ranges of acceptable execution times, or even divisions of time (such as "six times an hour"). To read up on these methods, see the man page in Chapter 5 (enter `man 5 crontab`).

NOTE: You can freely edit the system-wide `crontab` file
`/etc/crontab` to add schedule items outside individual
users' `crontab`s. The format of this file is similar to
that of other `crontab` files, except that it has an additional "who" field before the command column that's
used for specifying the user who is to execute each
command. Using this system-wide `crontab` file is generally considered suitable primarily for quick fixes; the
per-user `crontab` files are better security-wise, particularly for jobs executed as root.

Related to the `cron` scheduler is the `at` command,
which lets you execute one-time commands at a specified time.

Apple has disabled `at` and its related commands by
default because of how they might potentially interfere
with power management behavior. Read the `man at`
page for information on re-enabling the `at` command
and how to schedule a job to execute in the future.

Monitor System Performance

```
Activity Monitor
top -ocpu
```

Mac OS X gives us some pretty nice tools for figuring
out just what's going on with the system. If it seems to
be running sluggishly, or the disk seems to be making
lots of grinding noises, we don't have to guess at what's
going on—we can always just peek under the hood.

The GUI tool for monitoring system health is Activity
Monitor, found in the `/Applications/Utilities` folder.
This tool gives you a live-updating table of all the
processes in the system—not just the GUI applications—
sorted by how much CPU activity they're causing.

This way you can tell immediately if something is really sucking up the juice and kill it if you have to. Just select a suspicious process in the list and click Inspect to see more information about what it has been doing and what spawned it; or click **Quit Process** to send it a `kill -9` signal, the same as if you issued it a **Force Quit** command, as you saw earlier in this chapter.

Activity Monitor is really nice for this task, giving you all kinds of ways to slice and dice the running info about your system, seeing only those processes that are of interest to you or all processes, even in a hierarchical tree of inheritance; it even gives you separate displays for disk activity, system memory, network usage, and so on. But you don't always have the luxury of the GUI. Suppose, for example, that your system is so hosed that you can't get the Finder open to dig the Activity Monitor application out of the Utilities folder (you could always put it in your Dock, but that won't help you if you hadn't thought to do so in advance). Or suppose that you're logged in to your system through a remote SSH terminal. What then?

Well, then it's time to fall back on the good old-fashioned Unix tools: the `top` command (and the `-ocpu` option, which sorts the table by CPU usage):

```
Silver:~ btiemann$ top -ocpu
Processes:  90 total, 2 running, 88 sleeping... 309
Load Avg:  7.46, 4.31, 1.26    CPU usage:  91.1% u
SharedLibs: num =  207, resident = 41.8M code, 4.89
MemRegions: num = 25993, resident =  982M + 16.1M p
PhysMem:  194M wired, 1.03G active,  762M inactive
VM: 11.0G +  137M   339977(0) pageins, 198107(0) pa

   PID COMMAND        %CPU   TIME   #TH #PRTS #MREGS R
```

```
2468 dotmacsynnc  99.9%  0:01.71   1    18    22
  69 WindowServ    2.7%  3:23:38   3   562   954  9
 861 iTunes        1.7% 42:18.85   7   278   928  5
```

This output looks an awful lot like what Activity Monitor shows, huh? Granted, it's not as pretty, but it requires far less horsepower on the part of the system to get it fired up and tell you what's bringing your system to its knees (in this case, it's dotmacsyncclient, which seems to be stuck in some sort of infinite loop).

Some operating systems let you kill processes right from within top; Mac OS X seems not to have that capability. Instead, just take note of the process ID of the offending program—2468—and press Q to drop back to the command line. Now issue a kill command:

```
Silver:~ btiemann$ kill -9 2468
```

NOTE: You might need to use the sudo prefix to send kill signals to processes that you don't own.

A related and useful command is killall, which works like kill except that it takes a process name as an argument rather than a numeric process ID:

```
Silver:~ btiemann$ killall -9 dotmacsyncclient
```

Conclusion

Managing your applications is ostensibly the entire purpose of an operating system—removing obstacles between you and your data and then getting out of the way. At its best, a well-designed operating system fades into the background, and you never have to think about it. It's at those times when applications start to misbehave and no longer play by the well-established rules that a good operating system has the opportunity to step forward and become a great one. Reasonable people might disagree as to whether Mac OS X has really made that leap; but in comparison to what's come before it, and considering the balance it strikes between sophisticated GUI application management and nuts-and-bolts Unix tools, it gives the user more and better power tools than have ever been available elsewhere.

Working with Disks

Deep down, Mac OS X—like every other operating system—is about disks. From the days of the first consumer OSes published for desktop computers, the term *Disk Operating System*, or *DOS*, was at the heart of the vocabulary every computer owner had to know. The operating system was a mechanism for formatting, mounting, and navigating the floppy disks you could stick in your computer (in contrast to the cassette tapes and other clumsy media that preceded them). Running applications was almost a secondary function when it was amazing enough just to be able to store a novel's worth of text on a 5.25-inch square of plastic.

These days, *disk* is a term whose definition runs the gamut from traditional floppy disks (if you can still find any) to hard drives, Flash thumbdrives, CDs, DVDs, next-generation media such as HD-DVD and Blu-Ray, and even network volumes and virtual disk images. These kinds of media have different characteristics—some you can write to at any time, and some are session based, meaning you have to prepare a write session and then burn the whole thing to the disk in one shot. But they all share a common mission with the floppy disks that touched off the personal computer revolution almost 30 years ago.

NOTE: "Disk" is the generally accepted spelling for all kinds of removable and fixed media, except for optical media such as CD, DVD, HD-DVD, and Blu-Ray, which are spelled "disc." Thus, you'll find that most references to disks in Mac OS X spell it "disk," except for functions that are specifically optical-disc-related, such as "Disc Burning." In this book, I'll use "disk" as the generic term to encompass all types of storage media.

Volume can mean a partition of a disk, or it can mean an entire disk that has not been subpartitioned. As far as Mac OS X is concerned, every partition is its own separate device, even if several volumes are all carved out of the same hard disk. Anytime you see the word "volume," just think "disk" unless you're an expert at partitioning.

Monitor Disk Usage

```
Get Info
Activity Monitor
df
du
```

Mac OS X gives you a variety of means to keep track of your disk usage, some with more detail than others. Depending on your needs, you might be happy with the most easily accessible and least detailed views, or you might need a highly verbose analysis of where all your space is going. Let's look at a few of these in increasing order of both detail and obscurity.

First is the readout at the bottom of any Finder window. This will tell you two pieces of information: the number of items in the currently selected folder and the amount of free space on the disk or volume that it's on. To see the free space on a different disk, navigate to it or to a folder inside it in the Finder.

TIP: If you turn on the **Show item info** option in the **View Options** panel for a Finder window (or all windows), disks are labeled with a readout of the free and total space below the disk's name. This can be useful if you keep disks or aliases to them in common locations, such as on your desktop.

If, however, you need more info—for example, you need to know the exact number of bytes, not just the number of gigabytes rounded to the nearest hundredth, or if you need to know the used space as well as the free and total figures—you'll want to check the Get Info panel for the disk (select it in the Finder and select **File, Get Info**). Inside the **General** section you'll find a whole list of useful data, including the disk's format, when it was first formatted, and its usage numbers both in rounded-off gigabytes and in raw bytes.

Another option is to use the **Activity Monitor** utility (found in the Utilities folder inside Applications). At the bottom of its window is a **Disk Usage** section, which not only shows you the numbers for the usage of the disk you select from a drop-down menu, it also gives you a pie-chart view of how much of the disk is in use.

TIP: Have you suddenly noticed that you've got a lot less free space on your disk than you thought you had, and you can't figure out what's sucking it all up? It could be files sitting in your Trash or squirreled away inside bundles where even the Finder can't see them. To track down the items using the most disk space, try a utility such as the aptly named $10 shareware Where Is My Disk Space? (http://www.landsbert.dsl. pipex.com/diskspace/)

Finally, we must look at the command-line Unix utilities that provide similar functionality, often with more flexibility. The first such command is df, the "disk free" command:

```
Silver:~/Desktop btiemann$ df
Filesystem      1K-blocks      Used       Avail
   Capacity     Mounted on
/dev/disk0s9   245097216 187525828   57315388  77%  /
devfs          103         103        0   100%  /dev
fdesc          1           1          0   100%  /dev
<volfs>        12          512        0   100%  /.vol
automount -nsl [174]  0       0        0   100%  /Network
automount -fstab [181]  0     0        0   100%
   /automount/Servers
automount -static [181]  0    0        0   100%
   /automount/static
/dev/disk1s2       585948     268044     317904  46%
   /Volumes/iDisk
afp_3QlSxn3QlSxn3QlSxn3QlSxn-2.2c000007  348139820
➞248043134  100096686  71%  /Volumes/Scratch
   Disk
http://idisk.mac.com/btiemann/       2147483647
➞0 2147483647      0%  /Volumes/btiemann
```

This really opens up the hood of your system. It shows you not only the disks that are visible to the Finder (my startup disk, Macintosh HD, is the first entry in the list, known to the Unix system as /dev/disk0s9), but also several others that the system knows about but doesn't normally present to you. My iDisk, for example, shows up as a separate volume, as does the WebDAV-mounted, locally synchronized version of it (iDisk is a remote storage solution that is part of the $100/year .Mac service). There's also an entry for Scratch Disk, a remotely mounted network volume. The other items in this listing are there to support the automatic mounting system that attaches newly inserted or connected disks to the filesystem tree and places them under the /Volumes directory for Unix utilities to access them.

As you can see from the table, each disk is listed not only with the amount of free space (in 1-kilobyte units, or blocks), used, and available space, but also a percentage of capacity that can be an invaluable method for telling at a glance how full your disk is (no other method built in to the system gives you a percentage readout). My main disk is 77% full—I'd better think about upgrading before too much longer.

One more Unix utility to look at is du, the "disk usage" command. This tool lets you look at the amount of space taken up by a specific directory, either in summary or in detail. The du command can take a file, a list of files, or a directory name as an argument, but the simplest way to use it is to cd into the directory you want to summarize and then use du -s to get a complete, summarized readout, in kilobytes:

```
Silver:~/Desktop btiemann$ du -s
2301828  .
```

Wow—I've got 2.3 gigabytes on my desktop alone.
I'd better do some housecleaning.

If you omit the -s option, du will verbosely print out
the size of every subdirectory of the directory you
start from, which can help you zero in on where all
that space is going:

```
Silver:~/Desktop btiemann$ du
12       shoppinglist.pdf
Silver:~/Desktop btman$ du
328      ./Banzai.iMovieProject/Audio Waveforms
1440     ./Banzai.iMovieProject/Cache
2257040  ./Banzai.iMovieProject/Media
620      ./Banzai.iMovieProject/Shared Movies/Garage
620      ./Banzai.iMovieProject/Shared Movies/iDVD
1296     ./Banzai.iMovieProject/Shared Movies
2260184  ./Banzai.iMovieProject
7856     ./untitled folder
2301828  .
```

Ahh, right—that movie I was making in iMovie of my
dog Banzai chasing a laser pointer. That *was* about 2.3
gigabytes of video, wasn't it?

TIP: The -d option lets you specify a maximum depth
of subfolders to report. For instance, du -d 1 lets you
quickly and directly see which of the folders directly
beneath your current one is the biggest one:

```
Silver:~/Desktop btiemann$ du -d 1
    2260184 ./Banzai.iMovieProject
    7856    ./untitled folder
    2301828 .
```

You can also use the -h option to print the output in "human-readable" format, which means expressing the size values in terms of megabytes and gigabytes as appropriate.

Add a New Hard Disk to the System

Disk Utility
diskutil

Suppose you buy a new hard disk. You bring it home, you shut down your expandable tower Mac, and you install the disk in one of the spare drive bays (making sure to set the DIP switch settings according to the instructions on the drive and that came with your Mac). When you next power up the computer, you might expect to have to perform some esoteric formatting function, as is generally necessary on Linux. This isn't the case, however. Mac OS X will automatically recognize that a new and unformatted disk has been added to the system and will prompt you for instructions on what to do with it. You can enter a volume name, choose a filesystem format (**Mac OS Extended (Journaled)** is the default and best choice), and click **Initialize** to turn the disk into new usable space for your Mac.

Suppose, though, that you want to subpartition the disk into two or more volumes. To do this, and to perform many other disk operations, you need to cancel the dialog box that Mac OS X presented you with and launch **Disk Utility**, which is located in the Utilities folder (inside Applications).

All your computer's attached disks are shown in the pane at left. Unformatted disks (that is, disks that have not had any volumes created inside them) are shown as single icons with no subsidiary items; formatted disks each have at least one indented icon beneath them, each one representing a volume that the system recognizes as a separate disk. Suppose you want to divide your newly added disk into three sections (such as one for digital music, one for movie projects, and one for miscellaneous other stuff, each with its own partition that can't encroach on any of the others). To do this, select your newly installed disk (you can identify it by its manufacturer, capacity, and model number) and then select the **Partition** tab to the right. Choose **3 Partitions** from the **Volume Scheme** menu, and then drag the divider bars to set your three partitions to the sizes you want. Finally, click **Partition** to divide the disk into separate volumes, each of which appears in the list under its parent disk.

CAUTION: If you're partitioning a disk that will be used as a startup disk, you have to choose the correct partitioning scheme depending on whether you'll be booting PowerPC-based Macs (Apple Partition Map) or Intel-based Macs (GUID Partition Table). You won't be able to boot a Mac from a disk partitioned with the wrong kind of scheme. After selecting a volume scheme, click the **Options** button to choose a partition scheme.

Next, each volume needs to be formatted. Select each one in turn, choose the **Erase** tab, and specify a volume name and click **Erase** to format the volume.

This is also the method you'll use to reformat an existing disk. Any disk except for your startup disk can be erased completely with a reformat.

NOTE: If you're erasing a disk because you're selling your computer, or even just junking the hard disk, you might want to consider taking additional steps to ensure that any sensitive data on it can't be recovered by someone finding the disk in a dumpster. Identity theft is a growing threat in the digital age, as is digital blackmail—and I'm sure you can think of one or two things on your hard drive that you don't want someone selling back to you 10 years from now when you run for public office.

After a disk has been erased, go back into the **Erase** section and click **Erase Free Space**. This lets you choose from three types of scrubbing jobs: Zero out the data (useful only if the files have just been deleted, not if the whole disk has already been reformatted, and not foolproof even then), or a 7-pass or 35-pass erase that overwrites any existing data with random bits the specified number of times. If you have the time to spare, a 35-pass erase is the way to go if you want to be absolutely sure nobody will ever be able to get any juicy data off your disk.

TIP: You can even perform the secure Erase Free Space operation on a disk that's currently in use. It's a good idea for the security-conscious to do this from time to time, especially after erasing some particularly sensitive data. You can also securely scrub over files at the time you delete them by choosing **Finder, Secure Empty Trash** instead of plain **Empty Trash**.

CAUTION: Especially in the case of external USB or FireWire hard drives or Flash drives (including iPods), be sure to eject the disk in the Finder before disconnecting it. This ensures that any in-progress write operations are complete and the disk is still in a usable state when you reconnect it.

The `diskutil` command is the CLI-side utility for manipulating disks. It lets you mount, examine, modify, format, and perform many other operations on your disks and their volumes. See `man diskutil` for more information on this highly versatile tool.

Create a Disk Image

Disk Utility
`hdiutil create`

Disk images, as you learned in the previous chapter, are popular methods for software publishers to release their products for download over the Web. A disk image can be burned directly to an optical disc, which you can then store apart from your computer for safe-keeping. Installing an application from a burned disc is the same operation, as far as the system is concerned, as installing it from a mounted disk image: They're both just attached disks.

You might have need to create a disk image of your own, if you happen to be a software developer, or if you just want to archive some of your data in a standardized fashion, such as to make many copies of an installation CD or collection of files. To do this, you'll need to use **Disk Utility**.

First make sure that none of the disks or volumes in the left pane are selected; then click **New Image** in the toolbar. In the dialog sheet that appears, specify a filename and location to save the image, and pick a size. You're going to be creating a file that behaves like a virtual disk, including enforcing a size limit on what you can cram into it, so be sure to pick a size that's appropriate to what you plan to put in the disk image.

Several standardized sizes for CD-ROM and DVD formats are provided in case you plan to burn the disk image to disc.

TIP: If you select a disk or volume from the left pane before clicking New Image, Disk Utility will automatically create a disk image that's a clone of the selected volume. You can do this if you want to make a burnable copy of an entire volume.

There are two choices under the **Format** menu: read/write disk image and sparse disk image. The difference is that a regular read/write disk image is a file that takes up the full size you specify for the image, whereas a sparse image takes up only a minimum of space (about 11MB) plus the additional size of whatever items you add to it. This can be a useful consideration if you're short on disk space.

Finally, click **Create** to create the disk image. A file appears where you specified for the disk image to be created, and the system automatically opens and attaches (mounts) the virtual disk, just like any other disk you might connect to the system. You can then drag files into the disk to put duplicates inside the disk image file. The act of dragging an item into the disk automatically copies the item into the disk image file; no saving or burning is required. Eject the virtual disk when you're done with it.

On the CLI side, the hdiutil command gives you the functionality needed to create disk images. A sample hdiutil command for this purpose would be:

```
Silver:~ btiemann$ hdiutil create -size 50m
  image.dmg
```

More examples and options for hdiutil can be found in the **man hdiutil** page.

See the next chapter, "Burning a CD or DVD," for more information on how to burn a disc using a disk image.

Create an Encrypted Disk Image

Disk Utility
hdiutil create -encryption

Many users like to keep some of their data under encrypted lock and key, so that even if someone knows the user's login name and password (or comes upon a logged-in session on his Mac), he won't be able to access certain files without yet another password. The way that Mac OS X supports encryption for your files is by encouraging you to use disk images that are inherently encrypted using the AES-128 cipher.

Creating an encrypted disk image is essentially the same as creating a regular disk image (see the previous section); the difference is that when specifying the options for the disk image, you choose **AES-128** from the **Encryption** menu. Then, when you click **Create**, you're prompted to create a password for the disk image. As part of good security practice, this password should not be the same as your login password, and you should *not* allow Disk Utility to add the password to your Keychain (or else anyone with access to your login session would be able to open the disk image unchallenged, which defeats the purpose of this kind of security). Disable the check box for this option.

TIP: You can take advantage of Mac OS X's built-in password security advisor by clicking the key icon to the right of the first password field.

Now whenever you try to open and mount the disk image, you will be prompted to enter the password you specified. Be warned: There is no hint mechanism for this password. If you forget it, the data you put into the disk image is gone for good!

TIP: A somewhat more convenient and universal method for ensuring security for your data, particularly on laptops, is the **FileVault** feature, which you can turn on using the **Security** pane in System Preferences. When FileVault is turned on for your user account, your whole Home folder is encrypted and can be opened only using your login password. That way, you're never confronted with extra passwords to remember, and you can even set a master password that can regain access to your data even if you forget your own login password. But if your laptop is stolen, a thief won't be able to access your data even by taking out the hard drive and mounting it in another computer. FileVault does not, however, protect against someone walking by your desk and monkeying around with your login session—so make sure you've got a short timer and a password set on your screensaver!

The `hdiutil` command gives you similar functionality on the command line. Creating an encrypted disk image is just like creating a regular one, except with the addition of the `-encryption` option:

```
Silver:~ btiemann$ hdiutil create -size 50m
  -encryption image.dmg
```

Mac OS X pops up a graphical dialog box to prompt you for a password to use in locking the disk image. Note that this means you have to be working at the local terminal; you can't encrypt a disk image if you're logged in remotely (you'll get an "Authentication error").

More options, including predefined encryption types, can be found in the man `hdiutil` page.

Lock and Encrypt an Existing Disk Image

Disk Utility
`hdiutil convert`

Perhaps you created a disk image and put a bunch of files in it—but now you realize you want the disk image to be locked so no more changes can be made to it. Perhaps you also want to encrypt it, to protect sensitive data you've added. A disk image can be converted back and forth to an encrypted and/or read-only format using **Disk Utility**.

Select the disk image file in the left pane (all disk image files in the system are automatically tracked there) and click **Convert** in the toolbar. In the dialog sheet that appears, specify a name for the newly converted image file, and choose from the **Image Format** and **Encryption** menus whether you want the image to be locked (**read-only**) and whether you want it to be encrypted (using **AES-128**). Click **Create**; you'll be prompted for a password if you chose the encryption option. When the image is saved, it will contain all the data the original disk image had—but now it's immutable and unreadable by anybody but you. This same functionality is available in the `hdiutil` command, using the `convert` keyword. Specify the existing disk image name, the `-encryption` option, the `-format` option plus the `UDRO` string (which signifies "UDIF read-only"), and the output file name using the `-o` option:

```
Silver:~ btiemann$ hdiutil convert image.dmg
  -encryption -format UDRO -o image2.dmg
```

Mac OS X pops up a graphical dialog box to prompt you for a password to use in locking the disk image. Note that this means you have to be working at the local terminal; you can't encrypt a disk image if you're logged in remotely (you'll get an "Authentication error").

Many more image formats are available; refer to the **man hdiutil** page for more information.

Conclusion

The basics of disk operations are quite straightforward—more so, perhaps, in Mac OS X than in any other operating system. Where it gets really interesting, though, is when you start dabbling in the world of disk images, which use a whole different set of vocabulary from what methods you might be used to for accomplishing the same tasks on other operating systems. A little practice and familiarity, though, tends to illustrate pretty well why Apple's methods are disk-image–centric: It's a very flexible and elegant architecture, bringing together the world of online software distribution and burnable optical media, which segues neatly into the subject matter of the next chapter.

## 11

Burning a CD or DVD

Computing today has all but done away with the old iconography of the floppy disk in the striped shirt pocket. We don't put files on removable disks anymore; we email them to each other or stick them on web servers. About the only place we see floppy disks in any kind of useful role anymore is in much-loved but quaintly outdated geek movies like *Office Space*.

But we do still occasionally have a need to take our data with us. Whether it's an installer CD for an application, a DVD movie we created with a camcorder, or a playlist of favorite songs, we like to be able to burn our files to blank optical discs and take them with us. CD-Rs and DVD-Rs are session based, meaning that they don't have the immediacy and read/write flexibility of floppies—you have to put together a set of files to be written to the disc, and then burn it into the disc's surface in a single, fairly strenuous, one-time session that can't easily be undone. We've given up a lot of agility in the evolution to optical discs. What we've gained, though, is the capability to treat our data as disposable (considering how cheap blank optical discs are these days), as well as to have it interoperate with our CD and DVD players, as though we had recording and production studios in all our basements.

This chapter covers some of the common and uncommon operations you'll need to know about when preparing and burning optical discs.

Put Files on a Blank Disc

The first step in the process of burning a few files to a CD or DVD is simply to insert the blank disc. Mac OS X pops up a dialog box asking what you want to do with it: **Open Finder** is the typical response, although you can also choose to have it open in iTunes or in Disk Utility, and you can use the check box to **Make this action the default** for future discs you insert. (This can also be controlled in the CDs and DVDs pane of System Preferences, if you change your mind later.)

If you choose Open Finder, the blank CD appears on the desktop, labeled **Untitled CD** (I'm assuming you're using a CD-R here, not a DVD-R; if you're using the latter, the label will reflect that). You can change the label as you would any other item in the Finder, by clicking and typing.

Double-click to open the disc's Finder window. It looks a bit different from a normal Finder window, with a dark gray bar labeled **Recordable CD** and a **Burn** button at the right.

Now you can start filling up your disc with files. Drag in files, folders, or whole hierarchies of folders; arrange them on the disc the way you want someone opening your burned CD to see and navigate through them.

Notice that each item you drag into the Finder window appears with the little curved arrow in the lower left, indicating that it's a shortcut; this means that as you put files onto the temporary virtual disc that represents the blank CD in the system, it's not taking up any extra space on your hard drive.

Burn a Disc in the Finder

Burn Disc

When you're done setting up the contents of your recordable disc, it's time to burn those contents onto it, which is done at the same time as ejecting the disc and through the same mechanism: click and drag the disc icon from the desktop toward the Trash, as though you're going to eject it. Instead of a Trash can or an Eject symbol, though, you'll see the yellow-and-black **Burn** symbol. Drop the CD icon on top of this icon and the burn process begins.

TIP: A disc can also be burned by clicking the **Burn** icon next to the disc's label in the sidebar of the Finder, or by right-clicking the disc's icon and choosing **Burn Disc** (or choosing it from the **File** menu in the Finder).

First you see a dialog box where you can specify the disc's name (make sure to specify a label with fewer than 16 characters if the disc will be used in Windows PCs; similarly, avoid using special or nonalphanumeric characters in the name) and the burn speed (slower is more reliable, although you can usually make it as fast as it will go without any ill effects). Click **Burn** to write the contents to the disc, which consists of two parts—the burn itself and then the verification pass. Allow the verification to complete because, if the burn process went awry in any way, it will let you know of any nasty surprises that might await someone you give the disc to.

When the verification pass is done, the disc is mounted in the Finder, just like any other data CD-ROM or DVD. You just can't make any further changes to it.

NOTE: CD-RW and DVD±RW discs can ostensibly be rewritten, although support for this in Mac OS X is not especially direct and may not even be strictly possible. The way things are going, though, optical discs of any sort are getting cheap enough that you can just throw away a disc and use another. That's pretty much the reason why we all put up with session-based removable media anyway.

Save a Burn Folder

File → New Burn Folder

Mac OS X has a rather curious feature called *burn folders*. A burn folder is a set of files that you might want to burn to a CD, but that doesn't require you to have a disc actually inserted into the drive for you to set it up. You might use a burn folder if you want to prepare a burnable session of files but don't yet have the optical media handy yet to burn it to, or if you want to burn the same set of files to several discs for different people.

You can create a burn folder in several ways. The first is to choose **File, New Burn Folder** in the Finder. This creates a folder with the Burn symbol on it,

which, if you double-click it, looks like a recordable
disc's Finder window, with the dark gray bar over the
file list and the Burn button at the right. You can drag
files to it just as you would with an inserted CD-R or
writable DVD. When you're ready to burn discs from
the burn folder, click **Burn**; Mac OS X prompts you
to insert a new blank disc, and from that point the
process is the same as if you were burning a disc
directly as in the previous section.

Another way to create a burn folder is after the fact, at
the time you burn the disc. In the dialog box where
you specify the burning options, enable the **Save Burn
Folder To** check box, and specify a name for the burn
folder (the same as the disc's label by default). The
burn folder is created on your desktop, and you can
then proceed to burn more discs from it whenever you
want to.

Yet another way to make a burn folder is by inserting
a blank disc, dragging files to it, and then pressing the
Eject button on the keyboard. The disc is ejected without any complaint from the system, and the icon on
the desktop turns into a burn folder saved from the
disc's file set.

Make an ISO Image from a CD or DVD

```
hdiutil makehybrid -o mydisc /Volumes/Disc Name
```

One of the most common things people do with
blank discs is make copies of discs they own—whether
they're audio CDs, software installation discs, movie
DVDs, or anything else. Leaving aside questions of the
legality of duplicating discs (in this book, we'll assume

you're doing everything legally, of course), it's not entirely straightforward to do such a thing on the Mac, even if you've got a model with multiple optical drives. One typical way to duplicate a CD or DVD is to make an ISO image—an ISO9600-compliant bit-wise copy of the contents of an optical disc that has the necessary cross-platform formatting that allows it to be used on any operating system (hence the term *hybrid*). Then you can burn this ISO image to any number of discs and use them anywhere, on any machine you want.

Making an ISO image requires the use of a Unix command: hdiutil. This is an Apple utility that performs a great variety of disk operations, from mounting and unmounting disks to creating disk images, converting their formats, setting passwords and encryption, and so on. It's the underlying mechanism behind most of what Disk Utility does, as described in the previous chapter, but Disk Utility doesn't create ISO images. Only hdiutil does.

First, insert the disc you want to copy from. Suppose that Mac OS X mounts it using the label Disc Name. This means that it's mounted in the Unix filesystem as /Volumes/Disc Name; check that that's true by using ls.

Now, cd to the directory where you want the output .iso file to be created, and enter the following command, specifying the basename of the output file after the -o option:

```
Silver:~/Desktop btiemann$ hdiutil makehybrid -o
➥mydisc /Volumes/Disc Name
Creating hybrid image...
```

When this process is completed, you'll have a file called `mydisc.iso` in the same directory where you issued the command. This file is a cross-platform disc image that can be used on any operating system to create a new clone of the original disc. Pretty handy, huh?

TIP: You can make ISO images from any source—a hard drive volume, your iDisc, a mounted disc image, or even a folder full of files. Just specify the source file as the final argument in the command, making sure to address mounted volumes in their location within the `/Volumes` directory.

Burn a CD or DVD from a Disk Image

Disk Utility

Any type of disk image can be burned to a CD or DVD; that's pretty much their whole point. Whether it's a `.dmg`, `.img`, or `.iso` file you downloaded from the Internet or created yourself, Mac OS X treats them all the same—you can interact with the files in them by double-clicking and mounting them in the Finder, or you can burn them to discs using **Disk Utility** (in the Utilities folder inside Applications).

Because Disk Utility knows about all the disk image files that are present in your system, you'll see all such files in the pane at the left. (If the image file you want to burn doesn't appear there, drag the file from the Finder into the pane in Disk Utility.) Select the file that you want to burn; then click the **Burn** icon in the toolbar.

Disk Utility prompts you to insert a blank disc (eject-ing the tray if applicable), if one is not already present. After inserting the disc, click **Burn** to burn the con-tents of the disc image to the CD or DVD.

NOTE: Be sure to allow the verification process to fin-ish; you don't want to take the burned CD with you on the road and try to read some data from it, only to find out then that the disc didn't get burned properly.

Conclusion

The way Mac OS X interacts with burnable CDs and DVDs seems a bit schizophrenic to many—burning discs from folders or disc images isn't integrated into the Finder the way people expect who want to be able to right-click anything and send it off in an email, encrypt it, or burn a disc from it. However, you've got to think about the process in terms of the actual work-flow you're going to use: If you're going to burn a disc, the first step generally isn't to tell the system to burn a disc—it's to insert the blank disc to put stuff on it. After you know to start from that premise, the rest of the disc-burning mechanism starts to make more sense. Even burn folders look like a good idea after you've been staring at them for a while.

Disk Utility, as you've seen now in two chapters, is the center of your disk management life. The Finder is the casual-user navigation system, not the hard-core disk-image wrangling utility. If you're wondering how to do something with your disks and disk images that you're used to doing in the middle of Windows Explorer, fire up Disk Utility—chances are that it'll do what you're looking for and more.

## 12

Connecting to a Network

These days, a computer is hardly a computer without an Internet connection. Think about it: What applications do you use that don't involve the network at some point? Even apps like Word and Photoshop produce files that you usually expect to be able to transfer somewhere else, whether through email or web-based file sharing. Multimedia managers like iTunes and iPhoto, although they *can* work without a network connection, are missing a lot of their feature sets if your Mac isn't hooked up to a fat broadband pipe.

This chapter goes over the basic procedures for connecting your Mac to the network using the various methods available, as well as turning on the built-in firewall that will keep out unwanted traffic and potential exploiters of security holes.

Connect to a Wireless Network

Most Macs sold today are laptops, either MacBooks or MacBook Pros. All portable Macs come with wireless networking (known in the Apple world as AirPort) built in, and it's an option on all other Macs as well. All you have to do to get online with an AirPort-equipped Mac is be near an 802.11 (Wi-Fi) base station to which you have appropriate access.

The first step is to make sure that AirPort is turned on. Macs with AirPort installed have its status shown by default in the System Menus in the upper-right corner of the screen; the AirPort symbol is several concentric arcs, like radio waves. Click this icon to view a menu showing the AirPort status and the names of all wireless networks within range. Or, if AirPort is currently turned off, the icon appears as what looks like a pie slice; click this icon and choose **Turn AirPort On**.

TIP: If the AirPort icon is not visible in the System Menus, visit the **Network** pane of System Preferences and select **AirPort** from the **Show** menu to access the check box that controls whether the icon is shown in the menu bar.

If you see the name of the network to which you want to connect listed in the AirPort menu, select it. Otherwise, choose **Other** and, when prompted, enter the name of the hidden (closed) network you want to join.

Next, you might be prompted to enter a password. This is the key for Wired Equivalent Privacy, an encryption scheme used by most wireless networks to prevent casual snooping of the traffic flying through the air. It's not a particularly robust scheme and is fairly easily cracked, but it's still a virtual necessity for most networks to enforce some protection, even if just to keep unwanted users from joining the network and siphoning off its bandwidth (as in a hotel or airport). You'll need to know the WEP password and whether it's ASCII or hex, and enter it accordingly. Contact the owner of the wireless network for this information.

NOTE: Mac OS X remembers which wireless networks you've joined in the past and hangs on to their passwords, if you so desire, in your Keychain. That way, if it detects any of your trusted (previously used) networks in range, it will automatically connect to it using the saved password.

Finally, you might find that you still can't get online, even with the correct password. This might be because the wireless base station has limited access to its network on the basis of the Media Access Control (MAC) address, also known as the Ethernet or hardware address, a unique string of characters that identifies every networking device in the world. Different wireless base station makers implement this kind of control differently; Apple's AirPort Base Station series calls it "Access Control," whereas others might use terms such as "MAC addresses" or "Access list." Only if your computer's MAC address is entered in this list, and the base station restarted, will you be able to connect.

You can find your computer's MAC address by choosing **About This Mac** from the **Apple** menu, clicking **More Info**, and then clicking **Network** in the **Contents** panel. The MAC address is listed at the bottom of the page for each networking device you have in your computer.

TIP: You can also get the MAC address at the Terminal command line by typing `ifconfig en1` (the AirPort card

is generally the device called en1 on stock Mac
systems).

NOTE: Almost without exception, wireless networks are
configured to push TCP/IP configuration information
automatically to your computer through DHCP, so you
don't have to enter any IP addresses or anything yourself. If, for some reason, DHCP is not enabled on the
base station to which you connect, you'll need to configure your AirPort card's TCP/IP settings manually as
described in "Connect to an Ethernet Network with
Manual TCP/IP Settings," later in this chapter.

Connect to an Ethernet Network with DHCP

If you don't have an AirPort card, but you do have an
Ethernet cable and access to a hub or switch on a
home or business network, connecting to the Internet
can take one of two forms: the easy way (with DHCP)
and the hard way (without it). We'll look at the easy
way first.

When the Dynamic Host Configuration Protocol
(DHCP) is enabled on a local network, any computer
connecting to the network for the first time is automatically assigned an IP address from a pool of available addresses, and the TCP/IP configuration—from
the IP address and netmask to the gateway router and
DNS addresses—is automatically applied, giving you
full access to the network within a few seconds. There's
never more than minimal configuration involved with
hooking up to a DHCP network, and usually none.
Just plug in your Ethernet cable and see what happens.

Mac OS X is configured out of the box to try DHCP configuration first, and if it's not available, to fall back to manual configuration. If you didn't have a DHCP network available at the time you first set up your computer, or if your configuration has changed, you'll need to check your settings to make sure your computer is set up to look for a DHCP address. To do this, open the System Preferences and go to the **Network** pane; then choose your networking device (for example, **Ethernet**) from the device list on the left. Next, in the main pane, make sure that **Configure** is set to **Using DHCP**. Click **Apply** if any changes were necessary.

If all goes well, within a few seconds you'll see an IP address and subnet mask appear in the System Preferences window, along with a router address and DNS servers. When this happens, you can fire up your web browser and see if you can reach your favorite sites.

If something goes wrong—if, for example, your computer somehow misses the DHCP response from the server and doesn't get a proper address—you might see that your Mac gets an IP address that begins with 169.254. This is a "self-assigned" IP address, meaning that it just made it up for itself; this address has no bearing on the real-world network you're connected to, and you won't be able to get online with it. Try refreshing your DHCP information by clicking the **Advanced** button and then **Renew DHCP Lease** in the subsequent configuration page. If that doesn't work, contact your network administrator for assistance getting your Mac hooked up.

Finally, click **Apply** to finalize the settings and close the window.

NOTE: Mac OS X gives you several options for overriding the TCP/IP information given to you by the DHCP server. You can specify your own DNS servers or search domains, which are consulted before the ones provided by DHCP. In the **Advanced** configuration section, you can even choose **Using DHCP with manual address** from the **Configure IPv4** menu, meaning that you'll still get all your other TCP/IP information from the server, but you can specify your own manual IP address. Just make sure that this address is available and won't be assigned to someone else. Check with your network administrator to make sure about this before trying this option.

Connect to an Ethernet Network with Manual TCP/IP Settings

The traditional way to hook up to a corporate or university network is with an Ethernet cable and a set of esoteric but crucial TCP/IP numbers given to you by the administrator of the network. If this is how your network is set up, make sure you've got your machine's IP address, subnet mask, router address, and DNS server address before proceeding.

After plugging in your Ethernet cable to the appropriate port on your Mac, go into System Preferences and open up the **Network** pane. Choose **Ethernet** from the device list at left.

Set **Configure** to **Manually**. This makes all the remaining fields editable. Set the **IP Address**, **Subnet Mask**, **Router**, and **DNS Server** fields to the values given to you by your network administrator. If you were given a search domain, enter that, too. Finally, click **Apply**.

After you've done this, you should be able to connect to your favorite websites in your browser.

Connect to a Dial-up Network

If all you've got is a modem and a dial-up account, the Internet is bound to be a bit less of a fulfilling experience than it is for someone with broadband; but a slow connection is better than no connection at all, by any estimation.

To set up a dial-up connection, you'll need the account name, password, and phone number of your Internet Service Provider's dial-in pool. With this information in hand, connect your phone cord to your Mac (using either the built-in phone jack on older models or the external USB modem available for more recent ones) and open the **System Preferences**. Go to the **Network** pane and choose **Internal Modem** (or the appropriate modem by name, if your Mac doesn't have one built in) from the device list at left.

TIP: If you don't see your modem in the device list, or any other network device that you know you have installed, click the + button at the bottom of the pane and create a new service (device) using the modem, which you can select from the **Interface** menu. If your modem doesn't show up in that menu, the system might not be recognizing it properly, and you should seek technical support.

The two most interesting sections here are PPP and Modem. Under **PPP**, fill in as many of the fields as you can with the information you were given by your ISP; the required ones are the account name, password, and phone number. Optionally, you can also fill in the service provider's name (just to help you keep track of the configuration) and an alternate phone number if you have one. Enable the **Save password** check box if you want to be able to dial up without having to enter a password.

Click **PPP Options** to view a sheet with many configurable settings, such as how long the connection should be allowed to remain idle before it's automatically disconnected, whether the Mac should dial the modem automatically whenever any application needs access to the network, and so on. You likely won't need to worry about anything in the **Advanced Options** section, but anything above it you should feel free to experiment with to find the set of behaviors you're most comfortable with.

NOTE: Be careful with the **Connect automatically when needed** option. This will cause the modem to be dialed not only for checking your mail or uploading your iPhotos, but for seemingly trivial things like NTP automatically updating your system's time. If you've enabled any services that periodically try to contact the network, such as NTP or Software Update, don't enable this option unless you don't mind your computer occasionally dialing up the modem whenever it feels like it.

Now, in the Modem section, check to make sure that your modem's settings match your phone situation. Most particularly, consider enabling the check box to notify you when a phone call comes in while you're online. Also, the **Show modem status in menu bar** option is useful to enable—it gives you an easily visible indicator that tells you whether you're dialed up and for how long, as well as a convenient means to dial the modem and hang it up manually.

Finally, back in the PPP section, click **Dial Now** to test the configuration. If it successfully logs you in and establishes a connection, you'll be able to surf the Web in your favorite browser—slow though it might be.

Check Network Connectivity

Troubleshooting your Internet connection can be tricky if you're not versed in the intricacies of TCP/IP; even if you are, it's no slam-dunk. Sometimes you might fire up your browser and find that you just can't get anywhere without being confronted with the "You are not connected to the Internet" error page.

In the **Network** pane of System Preferences, all your networking devices are listed at the left side of the window, each with its connection status. Red and green lights indicate whether each device has a valid Internet connection.

Clicking on each device gives you additional details about its condition. The status messages that are reported for each device can vary a lot in format, but they give you all the information you need to determine what might be going wrong. For instance, a device using DHCP might show up as "active," but with a self-assigned IP address, which should indicate to you that it never properly got its TCP/IP settings. You should click that device to check the settings and possibly renew the DHCP lease. Or the light might be red, indicating that the Ethernet cable is disconnected, or that the AirPort card is turned off, or that WEP or base station access control has prevented your Mac from properly connecting to the network. Chances are that the high-level diagnostic overview presented on this page will get you on the right track to diagnosing your networking problem.

Protect Yourself with a Firewall

Any computer on the Internet is potentially at risk from malicious attackers. This goes for everybody: people behind a NAT router, people outside the usual DSL and cable IP address spaces, and even Mac users, believe it or not. Mac OS X may be pretty bulletproof compared to Windows, but it's just another Unix—and that means it might be running any of thousands of services, third-party or bundled, that might at any time be found to contain vulnerabilities to remote attack. Whether these vulnerabilities are plugged is usually up to Apple to fix, and even if they do release an update, you might not get that update in time before an attacker hits you with an exploit designed to take advantage of that vulnerability. But there is a saving grace: by running a firewall, denying remote access to any but the most fundamental of IP ports on your Mac, an attacker won't be able to reach the affected services in the first place, let alone to exploit an unpatched vulnerability.

The built-in firewall in Mac OS X is configured from the **Security** pane of the System Preferences, in (surprise!) the **Firewall** section. Start it up by changing the selected option to **Block all incoming connections** or **Limit incoming connections to specific services and applications**.

At this point, you should notice nothing different about your computer's behavior. The thing to remember about a firewall is that it prevents unsolicited *new* connections from outside from reaching your computer; but it won't block connections that *you* initiate, such as a request for a web page or an iChat conversation. The trick arises when you're running services that others might want to connect to, such as shared iTunes music or personal file sharing. For things like this, the solution is to create exception rules that match certain IP ports, allowing remote users to reach your computer through those ports. (You'll just have to hope that no vulnerabilities get unearthed on the services using those ports.)

Helpfully enough, Mac OS X provides you with a list of commonly accessible services to which you can allow access through the firewall. These services are not configured in the **Security** pane, though; rather, they're found in the **Sharing** pane, where you activate each file-sharing or resource-sharing subsystem individually by enabling its corresponding check box. As soon as each service is started, a hole is automatically opened in the firewall for any associated TCP or UDP ports on which external users might contact your Mac for that service. You'll see these activated services listed in the **Security** pane's **Firewall** section.

CAUTION: As a matter of good security practice, you should *only* enable those services that you're absolutely sure you need; this minimizes the number of ways that a newly discovered vulnerability might result in a way attackers can use to compromise your system.

Below the automatically configured resource-sharing services you can add individual applications that can be contacted remotely, such as iTunes and iChat. Different applications interact with the firewall in different ways. For example, to allow external users to share your iTunes music library, you would enable sharing in the Preferences window within iTunes; iTunes then automatically adds itself to your firewall's exception list, after confirming with a dialog box that you want to allow incoming connections. iChat also adds its own helper app to the firewall's rules when you first set it up, but it does so without prompting you for permission. In general, any application that might require you to open a hole in the firewall will do so on its own, through its own configuration process; this is the preferred method for adding applications to the firewall's configuration. However, if there's an application whose setup procedure does not automatically set up the firewall for you, you can add it to the list manually by clicking the **+** button below the list pane and selecting the app from the Applications folder.

The **Advanced** button gives you access to additional features, namely as **Enable Firewall Logging** (giving you detailed information about who's tried to get to your computer) and **Enable Stealth Mode** (preventing your Mac from even sending back a "connection refused" message to remote access attempts—it just ignores them entirely, making it look like you don't exist).

NOTE: If you're a Unix-head who's familiar with the use of the IPFW firewall (which is what Mac OS X uses), you can view the raw firewall rules with the `sudo ipfw show` command. But don't try adding your own rules at the command-line level, because they won't be saved for the next time your firewall is enabled, and the configuration for IPFW is kept in `.plist` files that are designed only to be written to by System Preferences.

Conclusion

TCP/IP networking is a vast and often academic topic, a full discussion of which is well beyond the scope of this book. This whirlwind tour through rudimentary TCP/IP configuration will give you only a "how-to" level of understanding of how it all works. If you're interested in reading more about how the IP address, MAC address, subnet mask, and router all work together to get your data packets from your Mac to some remote server and back, I'd suggest *TCP/IP Illustrated*, volume 1, by W. Richard Stevens (published by Addison-Wesley). This book is the bible of all networking professionals, and peering into its gritty yet elegant details might well prove fascinating. But even if not, hey, it looks impressive on your shelf.

## 13

Using Locations

Configuring TCP/IP settings is a pain. Even if you have DHCP and thus get all your networking settings automatically as soon as you hook up, you still face the prospect of having to change your settings if you switch from a wired to a wireless network or move from one network to another where different settings are required. Users don't want to have to muck around in the System Preferences every time they open up their laptops; they just want to get down to business.

Locations make this possible. A location is a saved set of networking preferences, including not just what kind of TCP/IP settings are required, but also which networking devices (such as Ethernet or wireless, or even modem, Bluetooth, or FireWire) are relevant to a certain physical environment. You can set up a location for work, another for home, and another for roaming for wireless hot spots; then, when you plug into a new network, getting connected is a simple matter of choosing the right location from the drop-down **Location** submenu in the Apple menu.

Create a New Location

Locations are configured in the **Network** pane of
System Preferences. A quick and in-context way to
get there is to go into the Apple menu, then the
Location submenu, and choose **Network Preferences**. (The **Location** sub-menu is only available if
you have more than one location configured.)

The pane on the left side shows you the status of all
the networking devices that you currently have configured, and none that you do not. You'll see how to
deactivate irrelevant devices later in this chapter. All
the listed *services* in that left pane, each of which is
the combination of an *interface* (such as Ethernet or
AirPort) with a TCP/IP configuration, along with
a service preference order, collectively comprise a
location.

In the default Mac OS X configuration, there's only
one location set up, called Automatic, which has
default services set up for all the interfaces in your
computer. This location is designed to connect your
Mac to any available networks by a hands-off method
as much as possible, first by trying to connect to any
open wireless networks it detects, and then to try connecting through a wired DHCP network if one is
available. These methods don't work if you have to
configure manual IP addresses, though, or if you want
to disable AirPort entirely in a wired environment.
Assuming this is the case for you, let's create a new
location called **Work**.

To do this, choose **Edit Location** from the **Location**
menu, and then click the **+** button at the bottom of
the location list. You're prompted to specify a name
instead of the default Untitled; enter **Work**, then click

Done. This new location now appears in the menu along with Automatic; its settings are cloned from those of Automatic. But now you can make whatever changes you like to the Work location, and Automatic will stay the way it was, allowing you to switch back to it when you go roaming with your laptop.

TIP: Rename or delete locations by selecting **Edit Locations** from the **Location** menu, then selecting the one you want to change and using the – button (to delete it) or the gear button followed by **Rename Location**. It's probably best not to delete Automatic, though; it really is useful as a universal fallback configuration.

Configure Network Settings for a Location

Now you can set up the Work location according to the specifications of your office network. As you saw in the previous chapter, set up your built-in Ethernet connection to use manual or DHCP-based TCP/IP settings, specifying internal DNS servers and other options as required by your system administrator. Similarly, set up your AirPort wireless connection to use the appropriate settings for your network.

NOTE: WEP passwords are stored in your Keychain and are not part of a specific location. Mac OS X will attempt to connect automatically to any networks within range that it has already connected to in the past and will use the saved password that you had already entered before.

The only trick is that you need to make sure that the location you're modifying is the Work one (keep an eye on the **Location** menu at the top of the window, which is always visible regardless of the section of the Network Preferences pane you're in). You don't want to alter the Automatic location so that it's no longer automatic.

Save the settings at any time by clicking **Apply**. From now on, selecting **Work** from the **Location** menu in the Apple menu switches you to your office's network architecture, and selecting **Automatic** switches you back to the open roaming mode.

Place Network Services in Preference Order

Here's where it really gets fun. Locations allow you not only to save environment-specific configurations for each of your devices, it allows you to specify the order in which Mac OS X should try them. For instance, you probably would always prefer a wired Ethernet connection over a wireless one, if one is available—wired Ethernet is much faster, much more secure, and doesn't use up extra battery power on your laptop. But if you're not plugged in at your desk, you still want to be able to get online. Similarly, if you have two networks available at the same time, you might want to be able to specify which one should have its TCP/IP settings take precedence—your wireless office network might be in a completely different address space or on a different security model than the wired connection at your desk.

From the gear button/menu at the bottom of the list of services in the Network Preferences pane, select **Set Service Order**. This lets you drag and drop all your available services (which, in the default configuration, are named after each of your available networking devices) into the appropriate order. Think carefully about what you want your computer to do, depending on what networks are available; Mac OS X will try the first service in the list first, and then if that fails, "fall through" to the next, and so on. For instance, you might think to yourself that you would prefer to use Ethernet if it's plugged in; but if it's not, then try AirPort. If so, you'd drag Ethernet to the top of the list.

Add and Remove Network Services

In the service list on the Network pane of System Preferences, red status lights indicate a disconnected or disabled networking device, such as an unplugged Ethernet cable or an AirPort wireless card that's turned off. However, the beauty of locations is that you can completely deactivate certain networking devices that you're never going to use in a given environment, such as your modem in your office network or your wired Ethernet port in a Starbucks. This prevents Mac OS X from wasting time trying to connect to a network that doesn't exist.

Suppose, for instance, that you know there are no wireless networks at your office (your Work location), and there's no point in connecting through a modem. You can select the AirPort and Internal Modem services in turn and click the — button at the bottom of the list to remove them completely. Similarly, you can turn on the Internal Modem setting for a location that describes a remote vacation home or the house you grew up in that still doesn't have broadband; you can put it at the bottom of the preference list if you want, to ensure that you'll connect through AirPort or Ethernet if they happen to be available, but the modem is always there as a last-resort fallback.

If you'd rather keep the services for less-used devices around, but prevent your Mac from trying to connect through them, you can use the **Make Service Inactive** option in the gear menu to turn AirPort and Internal Modem off, and they'll become grayed out for the location you have selected.

TIP: You can duplicate a service, making (for example) another version of your Ethernet device's configuration that you can define with a different set of TCP/IP information from your regular one, even within a single location. You can then choose the **Make Service Inactive** option to temporarily disable a service that doesn't apply to your current network environment. This is a good way to adapt your Mac to a rapidly changing network architecture without having to create a whole new location.

NOTE: You can delete network services as easily as you can create new ones, but be careful that you're modifying the location you really want to modify, and delete a service only if you're really sure you want it gone and wouldn't just rather deactivate in the locations where it's not relevant. You can re-create a service from scratch by clicking the **+** button and selecting the interface it pertains to, but don't take a chance on losing configuration information unless you're positive you know what you're doing.

Switch Locations as You Move

Now that you've got locations set up for all the different kinds of networking environments you'll be in, switching among them is the easiest part. Just choose the right entry from the **Location** submenu in the Apple menu. Allow a few seconds for the network settings to be applied.

TIP: As you saw in the previous chapter, it's a good idea for troubleshooting purposes to keep a Terminal window open so that you can use the ifconfig command to check what TCP/IP settings are being applied to your various interfaces. The en0 interface is typically Ethernet, and en1 is AirPort; you can use the ifconfig en1 command to view a specific interface's configuration or ifconfig by itself to see all your interfaces' settings at once.

NOTE: You can also switch locations by opening the **Network** Preferences pane, selecting a location from the **Location** menu, and clicking **Apply**. This is less direct, but gives you more visibility into what you're doing.

Conclusion

Locations are one of those features that made Mac OS X so endearing to networking professionals in its early years. Most operating systems now have functionality similar to it, but it's rare to find an implementation that's as seamless as the one in Mac OS X, after everything's set up to your satisfaction. Granted, the current design is still only a subset of the functionality that the classic Mac OS had—the equivalent to Locations in Mac OS 9 and earlier allowed you to configure localized settings for things like your system's audio volume and screen brightness, not just your various network devices—but in this day and age, networking is such an integral part of computing that the capability to so easily sort and selectively disable our devices based on networking environment is a pretty good consolation.

## 14

Sharing Files and Resources

One of the luxuries that Mac OS X inherits from being built on an open-source Unix platform is that it can speak all the networking languages that every other operating system speaks, because the open-source community has over the years developed solutions for allowing their Linux and BSD boxes to interoperate with the other machines on their networks. This means that not only can Mac OS X connect to AppleShare resources—shared from Macs using Apple's age-old networking protocol—it can also connect to Unix-native NFS shares, as well as to Windows-native SMB/CIFS shares using the open-source Samba utility. Using Mac OS X, you can even connect to WebDAV shares, such as iDisk. Mac OS X integrates all these protocols into the same set of functionality in the Finder, so that you don't even have to know what kind of share you're connecting to—they all work more or less the same way.

Allow Secure Remote Terminal Access

The most basic way to connect to any remote computer is through a text terminal, using either the clear-text Telnet or (as is fortunately much more common these days) the secure SSH, which stands for Secure Shell. When you use SSH to connect to a computer that supports it (which generally means a Unix machine), you get essentially the same kind of command-line environment you're now familiar with in the Terminal program on your Mac, and the same Unix commands work.

You'll see more about connecting to remote computers using SSH in the next chapter. For now, the goal is to open up your Mac so that you (or others you trust) can get access to it from a remote location, allowing you to manipulate files and run command-line programs on it no matter where you are.

NOTE: As with the other kinds of sharing protocols described in this chapter that can operate over routed IP networks, SSH is going to help you only if you connect to your Mac from a location that can access it directly by IP address. If your Mac is on a home network that uses Network Address Translation (NAT) to mask its true address range, you won't be able to use SSH to access your Mac from outside that local network.

Enabling SSH, though, is a piece of cake. You open up the **Sharing** pane of System Preferences and enable the check box in the **On** column next to **Remote Login**. With Remote Login enabled, any user who exists on your Mac can use SSH to connect to it remotely. For example, suppose the user "johndoe" wanted to connect to your Mac, whose IP address is 101.102.103.104. He would then enter the following Unix shell command:

```
Silver:~ john$ ssh johndoe@101.102.103.104
```

He'd be prompted for his password and would then be admitted to his Home directory on the command-line shell.

TIP: Graphical SSH programs, such as those that typically exist on Windows, often allow you to save SSH connection profiles so that a host can be reached with only a couple of clicks. When setting up a profile to connect to your Mac, the "johndoe" user would specify the username as **johndoe** and the IP address as **101.102.103.104** (or the hostname, if you have a resolvable DNS name assigned to your Mac). Be careful, however, of SSH programs that offer to save the password for you; unless the password is stored encrypted, as with an equivalent of the systemwide Keychain in Mac OS X or KDE, an attacker could find out John's password from his Windows SSH program and then gain unauthorized access to your Mac. Be sure you know who's connecting to your Mac and how they're doing it, and don't be afraid to deny them access if they're not being careful enough with your resources!

Mac OS X Leopard adds the new capability to specify a list of specific users who can access your Mac through SSH, rather than opening it up to every user on your system. To do this, change the radio button from **All Users** to **Only These Users**; then click the **+** button to select from a pop-up sheet that presents you with lists of all the groups and users on your system.

You can add individual users or whole groups (which you can set up in the **Accounts** pane of System Preferences) to the access list for Remote Login.

NOTE: Mac OS X in its default configuration does not support Telnet, the nonencrypted remote login program. Wisely, too, I might add—Telnet is highly insecure and a liability to any network and computer on which it's used.

Allow File Sharing by Other Macs

AppleShare (or AppleShare/IP) is the modern incarnation of the sharing protocol that has been used on Macs since they were 30 feet tall and plodded through the primeval jungles eating palm fronds. These days it's no longer a LAN-only protocol, and it can be routed over an IP network to any host that's reachable by direct address. This means that as long as your home network isn't behind a NAT gateway, you can mount your home Mac's hard drive onto your Mac at work and manipulate files on it as though it were an external hard drive you'd plugged in (albeit a really slow one).

First, though, you must set up your home Mac to share its resources. This is done in the **Sharing** Preferences pane, using the **File Sharing** service item. Click the **On** check box, which sets up the basic Personal File Sharing service, which shares items to remotely connecting users as follows:

- **If the user connects as a Guest (no password required)**, the user has read-only access to every user's Public folder on your Mac and can place items into the Drop Box folder inside it, although the user cannot open the Drop Box folder to see what else is inside it.

- **If the user connects as an authenticated user**, the user has the choice to mount either his or her own Home folder or the entire computer's hard drive or any other mounted disks. Full read/write access is granted on either of these resources if you allow it for that user, but Unix-level permissions are still in effect, so remote users will not be able to modify any items they do not own, such as system files.

You can set up additional shared folders beyond these, if you so desire. Use the **+** icon under **Shared Folders** to choose folders to share, and then use the **+** icon under **Users** to specify local users and groups who should have access to each shared folder you specify, as well as tuning each one to have read-only or full read/write access. When a user attempts to connect to your Mac over AppleShare, each shared folder to which that user has been given access will appear as an available choice to mount over the network.

Allow File Sharing by Windows Computers

Windows users can connect to the same shared resources on your Mac as Mac users can, using the SMB (or CIFS) protocol that is native to Windows rather than the Mac's AppleShare protocol. This is made possible using the open-source Samba package that has provided Windows sharing functionality on

Linux and other Unix-type systems for many years. However, one drawback of Samba is that it requires its own separate user database, distinct from the one used for the host system's native login authentication, because Windows-style authentication uses a different method for encrypting its passwords. Because the Samba user database is kept under lock and key and can be modified only through an administrative action, the only way to set up this separate password database is for you to enter each user's password into the algorithm that encrypts it for Windows, thus enabling that user. The upshot of this is that before any of your users can connect from a Windows machine, you need to enable each one individually, entering each user's password at the time you do so.

In the **Sharing** Preferences pane, select **File Sharing**, and then click **Options**. A dialog sheet appears that gives you the option to enable and disable the **Share files and folders using SMB** check box, as well as to enable each local user to access your system. Click the **On** check box for a user and enter that user's password when prompted to enable that user.

After a user has been enabled, anyone connecting from a Windows machine can do so by accessing the Windows-style SMB/CIFS path \\101.102.103.104\ johndoe (for a user called "johndoe" accessing his Home folder on your Mac at the IP address 101.102.103.104), or—if you want to be really twisted—from a Mac, using the URL-style address smb://101.102.103.104/johndoe. You'll be prompted for a valid username and password, after which the shared folder will appear as a mounted remote disk on the Windows machine.

TIP: By default, Mac OS X has no predefined Windows workgroup name or WINS server, but you can set these options to conform to your network environment. Go to the **Network** Preferences pane, then click the **Advanced** button in the lower right of any service's configuration pane. The resulting dialog has many useful tabs, one of which is **WINS**. Under this tab, you can specify a workgroup name (allowing your Mac to show up in that workgroup on the Windows network) and add WINS server IP addresses (to allow you to browse the Windows network's computers by name).

Connect to a Shared Disk Resource on a Mac

```
afp://101.102.103.104
afp://user;AUTH=authType:password@server-
name:port/volume-name/path
➡mount_afp
```

Suppose there's a share disk resource on a Mac somewhere that you want to connect to—your Mac at home or another Mac on the office or university network. How do you connect to it?

There are several ways. The most user-friendly case is the one where the resource is shared from a computer on the same local network, which means you can browse to it by name. Do this by selecting **Network** from the **Go** menu in the Finder. In the resulting Finder window, you'll find all the AppleShare servers advertising their availability on the network, and you can choose the right one by its name. You'll see all the publicly available shares listed immediately under the server's name (Mac OS X connects automatically to the server as soon as you browse into it), and you can navigate into each share just as you would any folder. If there are shares on the server that can only be reached by registered users on that server, click **Connect As** to be prompted for authentication. After you've done that, the list of available shares changes to the more generous set that registered users get (generally any complete disk on the system, as well as your own home folder).

NOTE: When you connect to any shared resource, it becomes mounted on your system like an external disk. Mac OS X streamlines this process for Apple-Share servers, hiding the mounted shares and aggregating them under the server's name in the Finder's sidebar; but you should always "eject" a share when you're done using it, especially if you're using a laptop. Otherwse, if you move to a location where the still-mounted share can't be reached, system sluggishness can result while the Finder tries to reestablish the link to the share.

TIP: All shared resource servers are listed under the Shared heading in the Finder's sidebar. You can navigate directly into a server's shares using that shortcut.

The other, more general, way to connect to an AppleShare resource is by URL. This way is a lot more direct if you happen to know the IP address or hostname of the file server, and it also allows you to connect to Macs that aren't necessarily located on your same local network. This is how you would connect from work back to your Mac at home, for example.

In the Finder, choose **Go**, then **Connect to Server**
(⌘+K). In the **Server Address** field, enter an
AppleShare Filing Protocol address like this:

```
afp://101.102.103.104
```

Then click **Connect**. After a few seconds (depending
on the speed and responsiveness of the network), you'll
be prompted to authenticate and pick a resource to
mount, just as if you had browsed for the share in the
Finder.

More complex URLs can get you into shares that are
open to registered users only. For example, to connect
to my home folder on the server, where my username
is "btiemann" and my password is "abc123", I would
use a URL like the following:

```
afp://btiemann:abc123@101.102.103.104/btiemann
```

If you omit the username or the password, you will be
prompted to enter them. The general form of the AFP
URL, including the optional fields to specify an alternate authentication mechanism or a non-standard
TCP/IP port, is:

```
afp://user;AUTH=authType:password@server-name:
➥port/volume-name/path
```

TIP: Before clicking **Connect**, you can use the **+** button
to add the server URL to your **Favorite Servers** list,
making it easy to reconnect to the same server in the
future by clicking it in the list.

TIP: You can automatically mount any share at login, by mounting it and then adding the mounted disk icon to your **Login Items** list in the **Accounts** pane of System Preferences. If you've saved the password for mounting the share in your Keychain, the share will appear on your desktop as soon as you log in each time.

Another way to quickly return to a mounted share is to make an alias to it, either on your desktop, in your Finder's sidebar, or by dragging it to your Dock. When you unmount the share, the alias doesn't disappear; a double-click (or single-click in the Dock) brings it right back.

Finally, it's possible to mount an AFP share using the Terminal command line only. This method gives you more flexibility, such as the ability to mount a share anywhere in the system, such as within your home folder. You do this using the same URL mechanism described earlier, but with the mount_afp command:

```
Silver:~ btiemann$ mount_afp
afp://btiemann:abc123@101.102.103.104/
btiemann~/Silver
```

The final argument specifies a folder where you want to attach the remote share. This folder must already exist before you try to mount the resource, and it should be empty (because its contents become temporarily replaced with the share's). Also, if you omit the username and password, mount_afp will attempt to connect as a guest, and fail if that doesn't work; you don't get a dialog prompting for the credentials. Finally, note that Unix permissions apply, so if you want to mount the share somewhere where you don't have write permission, you'll need to precede the command with sudo.

Connect to a Shared Disk Resource on a Windows Computer

```
smb://101.102.103.104
mount_smbfs
```

These days, it's a lot more likely—especially in an office environment—that the shared resource you want to connect to is on a Windows file server, shared over SMB/CIFS, the native Windows sharing protocol. No matter—Mac OS X speaks SMB, whether it's for sharing its own resources with Windows users, or the other way around.

Windows file sharing is conceptually very much like AppleShare and works in the same two ways: either you can browse for the file server you want on the local network, or you can address it directly by URL. If you're browsing in the Finder, select **Go, Network**, and then browse into the folder representing the workgroup or domain of your Windows network. Inside, you'll find a list of all the Windows file servers advertising their services (this might include Linux machines running Samba, or even Macs with Windows Sharing enabled). Select one and click **Connect** to pick a shared resource and authenticate for access.

NOTE: To specify a workgroup name other than the default, WORKGROUP, open the Network Preferences panel, click **Advanced**, and go to the **WINS** tab.

TIP: You can join your Mac to a Windows domain and be automatically authenticated to access any Windows share on the network. To do this, launch **Directory Access** (located in your Utilities folder), select **Active Directory** under **Services**, and click **Configure**. You can then enter the domain name and your computer's ID as recognized by the central domain controller (your network administrator needs to explicitly add your Mac to the network before you can bind to the domain), and click **Bind**.

You can also use a direct URL to mount a Windows share by choosing **Go**, **Connect to Server**, and entering the following in the **Server Address** field:

```
smb://101.102.103.104/johndoe
```

You'll then be prompted for a valid username and password, after which the shared folder will appear as a mounted remote disk on the Windows machine. Alternatively, you can leave off the johndoe part at the end of the address, and you'll be prompted to select the shared resource to connect to before being prompted for your authentication details (if you're not bound to a domain already).

TIP: If you're in a domain, and you want to connect to a share that uses different authentication privileges than are enforced by the domain, you can click **Authenticate** rather than **OK** to enter the appropriate credentials.

TIP: As with AFP, you can avoid the authentication dialog by specifying the username and password in the URL directly, with this syntax:

```
smb://btiemann:abc123@101.102.103.104/johndoe
```

Just as with AFP, you can use the `mount_smbfs` command in the Terminal to mount an SMB share manually in a location you specify:

```
Silver:~ btiemann$ mount_smbfs
smb://101.102.103.104/johndoe ~/Silver
```

Connect to a Shared NFS Resource

```
nfs://101.102.103.104/path/to/share
mount_nfs
```

NFS, the Network File System, is the venerable Unix way of sharing files on a network. NFS shares work in much the same way that AppleShare and SMB/CIFS shares do, except that there's no authentication built in. NFS access control is done at the network level, allowing or denying hosts on the basis of their IP addresses or hostnames. Before connecting to an NFS share, make sure you're supposed to be able to access it—you don't want to beat your head against a wall trying to get Mac OS X to mount a share properly when it turns out that you were never given proper access at the server level.

Conceptually, mounting an NFS share is pretty simple: You have one option for specifying the resource's location, a URL (which you enter in the **Server Address** field in the **Connect to Server** dialog box):

```
nfs://101.102.103.104/path/to/share
```

This causes a share labeled **share** to appear on your desktop.

NOTE: NFS has no built-in browse functionality; this means you normally can't locate an NFS server by poking around in the Network section in the Finder. Some networks, however, are running SLP, the Service Location Protocol, which broadcasts the names and locations of NFS resources on the network. If you have an SLP-enabled network, you'll be able to browse for NFS shares just like other types of network resources.

TIP: You can use the technique described earlier in this chapter to automatically mount an NFS server at login time, just like the other kinds of shares. But if you want the share to be mounted at boot even without you having to log in (a useful trick if you're using your Mac as a server), you can use the **automount** service as described here:
http://www.oreillynet.com/pub/h/341

Just as with AFP, you can use the `mount_nfs` command in the Terminal to mount an NFS share manually in a location you specify:

```
Silver:~ btiemann$ mount_nfs
nfs://101.102.103.104/path/to/share ~/Silver
```

Connect to a WebDAV Resource

```
http://server_name/path/to/share
mount_webdav
```

WebDAV is a newer sharing protocol that operates over HTTP, giving people the capability to upload and edit resources on the server side. It has been growing in popularity lately for applications such as shared calendaring and contact directories, and it's the underlying technology of Apple's .Mac service. In fact, if you have a .Mac account and you use the iDisk remote-disk functionality, you're using WebDAV already.

Your network might have a WebDAV server set up for calendaring or file-sharing purposes. If so, you can connect to it by URL, like any other resource. Supposing the WebDAV server is on a host called antares, all you have to do is specify the URL in the **Connect to Server** window:

```
http://antares/path/to/share
```

This prompts you for authentication, if necessary, and then mounts the share resource on your desktop like any other.

TIP: WebDAV normally runs on the default HTTP port, 80; but if it has been configured to use a nonstandard port, you can specify it using a URL like the following: http://antares:1984/path/to/share

---

Just as with AFP, you can use the mount_webdav command in the Terminal to mount a WebDAV share manually in a location you specify:

```
Silver:~ btiemann$ mount_webdav
http://antares:1984/path/to/share ~/Silver
```

Connect to an FTP Server

```
ftp://ftp.example.com/path/to/resource
```

FTP, the File Transfer Protocol, is one of the oldest applications on the Internet still in wide use today; it's not really a "sharing" protocol that emulates a filesystem the way AppleShare and SMB/CIFS and NFS are, but rather a means for transferring large files back and forth on a command-driven, client/server basis. Authenticated at the system login level and supporting much finer-grained control than protocols such as NFS, its versatility has helped keep FTP in currency even though its unencrypted nature makes it as much a liability on secure networks as Telnet is.

You'll see in the next chapter how to use the command-line version of FTP, which is arguably more efficient than the GUI variety that Apple has integrated into Mac OS X's file-sharing architecture. Here, though, we'll go over the way to connect to an FTP server in the Finder, a method that conflates FTP with a resource-sharing mechanism—something it's really not intended to be, but a capacity in which it can be made to function if necessary.

As with the other kinds of shared resources, the way to connect is by entering a URL in the **Connect to Server** window:

```
ftp://ftp.example.com/path/to/resource
```

If the FTP server is configured for anonymous (guest) access, the resource will appear mounted on your desktop, labeled with the server name, like any other share. Otherwise, you'll be prompted for a username and password for authenticated access.

TIP: As with AFP, you can avoid the authentication dialog by specifying the username and password in the URL directly, with this syntax:
```
ftp://btiemann:abc123@ftp.example.com/path/to/
resource
```

Navigating an FTP share is where things get a little bit tricky. Because FTP is not meant to work like a filesystem, you might find that items that look like they can be downloaded or accessed actually can't be, or you might try to upload an item by dragging it into the window only to meet with an odd error message. Navigation might be slow or clumsy. Well-behaved servers can be a joy to work with in this way, but unresponsive ones are even more finicky than sluggish NFS or SMB servers. See Chapter 15, "Command-Line Networking Tools," for an introduction to command-line FTP, which might prove more appropriate to your needs, and SCP, which gives you encrypted file-transfer capabilities on a secure network.

NOTE: You can set up your Mac to allow others to transfer files to and from it using FTP. This is accomplished in much the same way as turning on SMB file sharing: in the **Sharing** Preferences pane, select **File Sharing**, then click **Options**. Enable the check box for **Share files and folders using FTP**. Be aware that this means your users will be transmitting their passwords for logging into your Mac in the clear.

Just as with AFP, you can use the mount_ftp command in the Terminal to mount an FTP share manually in a location you specify:

```
Silver:~ btiemann$ mount_ftp ftp://btiemann:
➥abc123@ftp.example.com/path/to/resource ~/Silver
```

Disconnect from a Shared Resource

When you're done using any shared resource, you can unmount it from your Mac to disconnect from it. This isn't strictly necessary—you can also just leave it connected, or let your Mac go to sleep, or disconnect from the network and the shared resource won't suffer any ill effects—but to avoid getting warning messages about servers unexpectedly disappearing, and to keep your desktop tidy, it's a good idea to disconnect when you're done working with a share.

Disconnecting works just the same as unmounting any disk or volume: Click the **Eject** button next to its icon in the Finder's sidebar, or drag the share to the Trash (which turns into an Eject symbol while you're dragging).

Conclusion

There are seemingly as many ways to share files on the Internet these days as there are operating systems, if not more. Fortunately, Mac OS X provides a more-or-less unified interface that brings them all together using the same metaphors, so that from a user's standpoint there isn't any significant difference between AppleShare, SMB/CIFS, NFS, or anything else that has yet to be dreamed up.

## 15

Command-Line Networking Tools

We're all used to using high-tech, full-featured, polished-to-a-high-gloss web browsers to do our navigating about the Web these days. But all but lost under all the modern bells and whistles are the reasons why people have been using the Internet for almost 30 years now: to transfer files back and forth and to run programs on remote computers from our own terminals.

Modern tools can do these things, true; but they're often so heavyweight and so artificially user-friendly that they actually get in the way of the tasks we really want to perform. As it turns out, then, there's still a place in today's Internet for the venerable command-line Unix utilities that people have been using for decades to download and upload files, unencumbered with all the trappings of the drag-and-drop, icon-driven world we live in today.

Check Network Connectivity with Ping

```
ping hostname
```

Perhaps the most common reason for a Mac user to dig out the Terminal from its hiding place in Utilities is to run Ping, a simple utility whose purpose is to check whether a certain host on the Internet is reachable from your computer. More often than not, it's used to tell you whether your computer's networking has been set up correctly; if you try to ping a server that you know is up and running, then the results of Ping tell you right away whether your own machine is on the network properly or not.

```
Silver:~ btiemann$ ping www.apple.com
PING www.apple.com.akadns.net (17.112.152.32): 56
data bytes
64 bytes from 17.112.152.32: icmp_seq=0 ttl=241
time=20.173 ms
64 bytes from 17.112.152.32: icmp_seq=1 ttl=241
time=23.188 ms
64 bytes from 17.112.152.32: icmp_seq=2 ttl=241
time=16.893 ms
```

Ping runs continuously until you press Ctrl+C to stop it (unlike the Windows version of Ping, which sends four attempts and then quits). Each line represents an ICMP packet that travels to the remote host (which you can specify by hostname or by IP address), then returns with information about how long it took. Thus Ping can tell you not only whether the host is alive and responding, but how congested the network conditions are between you and that host.

> **NOTE:** If Ping returns messages such as "Host unreachable" or "No route to host," and if you're sure that the host you're pinging is reachable (that is, you can reach it from another computer), it probably means that your Mac's networking is not configured properly.

Trace the Route to Another Computer with Traceroute

```
traceroute hostname
```

Using the same ICMP technology as Ping, the Traceroute command follows the path from router to router that it must travel to get from your computer to another given host, and sends back a status message for each hop along the way. This information tells you how responsive the network is each step of the way, helping you to diagnose network problems, as well as giving you geographic clues as to where exactly in the world your traffic is going.

```
Silver:~ btiemann$ traceroute ntp.org
traceroute to ntp.org (128.4.35.16), 64 hops max,
➡40 byte packets
 1  10.0.1.1 (10.0.1.1)  1.164 ms  0.749 ms  23.228
ms
 2  ge-2-21-ur03.sanjose.ca.sfba.comcast.net
➡(68.87.197.229)  23.524 ms  17.548 ms  9.021 ms
 3  COMCAST-IP.car2.SanJose1.Level3.net
➡(4.79.43.138)  17.273 ms  17.822 ms  18.643 ms
 4  te-4-3.car2.SanJose1.Level3.net
➡(4.79.43.137)  23.565 ms  19.492 ms  39.638 ms
```

```
 5  ae-23-79.car3.SanJose1.Level3.net
➡(4.68.18.69)  13.842 ms  22.024 ms  18.021 ms
. . .
16  UD.demarc.cogentco.com (38.112.5.86)
➡95.591 ms  92.662 ms  95.942 ms
17  chp-rt2-v9.nss.udel.edu (128.175.111.10)
➡96.808 ms  96.723 ms  104.321 ms
18  host-137-2.nss.udel.edu (128.175.137.2)
➡106.345 ms  104.268 ms  94.351 ms
19  128.4.40.64 (128.4.40.64)  100.960 ms
➡104.453 ms  94.075 ms
20  128.4.35.14 (128.4.35.14)  110.877
➡ms dewey.udel.edu (128.4.40.11)  114.772 ms
  92.516 ms
```

Three probe attempts are made at each step of the way, and the time each one takes to reach is reported. If you see timeouts (indicated by asterisks, for example a line consisting of "* * *"), that means the route has reached a dead end, and the host you're trying to reach either can't be contacted, or is blocking ICMP (a common practice in secured networks).

Connect to a Remote Mac or Unix Computer Using SSH

```
ssh username@remote_host
```

When you connect to a remote server's command line, you'll find yourself in the same kind of environment as you'd get running Terminal on your own local Mac. You can list files with ls, monitor system processes with top, use text editors, perform administrative tasks—in short, do everything you could do sitting in front of the computer, with the exception of safely reconfiguring the network or switching the computer back on if it gets turned off. The best part is that it's all done through text, so there's hardly anything that gets sent over the network—far less than all the graphics that would be necessary to transfer and track if you were trying to view a remote computer's GUI.

This location-agnostic versatility is brought to you by SSH, the Secure Shell. All communications over SSH take place in an encrypted "tunnel," so that even if someone is snooping on your network traffic, he won't be able to tell what you're typing. This is what makes SSH far preferable to the older, unencrypted Telnet, which was nothing short of an invitation to intercept usernames and passwords on their way to the remote server.

To connect to a remote host (`regulus.example.com` in this example) using SSH, use the following shell command:

```
Silver:~ btiemann$ ssh btiemann@regulus.example.com
```

With this syntax, you can specify the username you want to connect as (which has to exist on the remote system). If the remote host has the same usernames as exist on your local Mac—if, for example, the remote username is `btiemann` and my local Mac's login account is `btiemann`, I can skip the username part and use this simpler syntax:

```
Silver:~ btiemann$ ssh regulus.example.com
```

NOTE: If this is the first time you've connected to a given remote host, you're prompted for whether you want to save the host's fingerprint in your `.ssh/known_hosts` file. This fingerprint is used for security, ensuring that the remote host's fingerprint is always the same every time you connect. If the fingerprint changes, it could mean that someone else is posing as the server you're trying to connect to and is trying to steal your password. SSH will notice if this happens and prevent you from connecting unless you're sure the fingerprint has changed for a good reason (such as if the server's operating system has been reinstalled). If this is the case, you need to edit the .ssh/known_hosts file and remove the line corresponding to the remote host in question so that a new fingerprint can be entered the next time you connect.

You're then prompted to enter your password. **Note:** your password is not echoed to the screen as you type it! It might look like nothing is happening, but trust me—what you're typing *is* being transmitted. Just type it blindly and press Return. Assuming that you entered the password correctly, you're deposited at the remote computer's command line, where you can issue any of the universal Unix commands you learned about in earlier chapters of this book, which will usually work (with only a few minor variations) on other types of systems, such as Linux and FreeBSD and Solaris.

Type **exit** to log out of your SSH session.

NOTE: The Terminal application normally prompts you for confirmation if you try to close a window where a process is currently running, such as top. But Terminal is smart enough to know that certain commands that you enter mean that you're going off into another command-line mode that shouldn't stop you from closing the window; these commands are listed in the **Shell** section of the **Settings** tab in Terminal's Preferences and you can add to the list or modify it as you see fit.

Transfer Files Using FTP and SFTP

```
ftp
sftp
```

You saw in the previous chapter how to use FTP in the Mac OS X GUI, as though it were a file-sharing protocol like AppleShare or NFS. It was never intended as such, though, and sometimes you might find that it's simpler and more efficient to use the command-line FTP program to download or upload files.

Working with FTP is a lot like working with the Unix command line itself. Many of the commands for listing files and manipulating folders are the same. There are a few tricks to keep in mind, however, and you'll see them as part of the procedure.

The first step is to fire up a Terminal window and put yourself in the directory where you want to download files to (or upload them from). We'll use the desktop for this example.

```
Silver:~ btiemann$ cd Desktop
```

Now enter the FTP program, giving it the hostname or IP address of an FTP server to which you want to connect:

```
Silver:~ btiemann$ ftp ftp.example.com
Trying 204.152.184.73...
Connected to ftp.example.com.
220 Welcome to ftp.example.com.
Name (ftp.example.com:btiemann):
```

Now comes the authentication step. If you have a username and password on the remote server, enter those as prompted; otherwise, as is usually the case for public file distribution servers, you need to connect in anonymous mode, by entering either **anonymous** or **ftp** as the username. For the password, enter your email address. (This is usually not validated in any way; it's just a courtesy, to let the server owner know who you are.) You're then dropped into the ftp> prompt.

You can now list files on the server with ls, change directories using cd, and even (if you have appropriate permissions) create directories with mkdir and **delete** items with del (not rm). The commands you'll most want to know about, though, are put (upload) and get (download).

```
ftp> get tarball.tar.gz
local: tarball.tar.gz remote: tarball.tar.gz
229 Entering Extended Passive Mode (|||38776|)
150 Opening BINARY mode data connection for
➥tarball.tar.gz (40227 bytes).
100% |*************************| 40227      454.98
KB/s    00:00
226 File send OK.
40227 bytes received in 00:00 (336.81 KB/s)
```

NOTE: Most FTP servers operate by default in binary mode these days, meaning that files are sent with no translation of end-of-line characters, assuming that the files you're transferring are binary and need no such translation. Translation is necessary only if you're transferring plain-text files between unlike operating systems, in which case you can change to ASCII mode with the asc command. In general, though, use the bin command right after connecting to make sure you're in binary mode, which is generally safest (your Mac is the same kind of OS as most FTP servers, so no translation is necessary).

Use the quit, exit, or bye command to quit FTP when you're done. It is, after all, just an application—not a mounted filesystem, the way the GUI pretends it is.

Note that FTP is a clear-text protocol, meaning that all your communications with the server—including usernames and passwords—are transferred unencrypted. If the remote server supports it, you can use the sftp command instead of ftp; it uses the secure channel provided by most SSH installations to provide the same functionality you expect in an interactive FTP session.

```
Silver:~ btiemann$ sftp ftp.example.com
```

Transfer Files Securely Using SCP

```
scp username@remote_host:/path/to/file
path/to/local/destination
scp path/to/local/source
username@remote_host:/path/to/remote/destination
```

As convenient as FTP is, it's unsecure; there's no encryption protecting the data from snoopers, and if you're not using anonymous logins, you're sending your username and password over the network in the clear. That's a big no-no. Furthermore, the SFTP protocol might not be available on the remote server, or you might not want to go through the interactive steps necessary to use it. You might simply want to transfer a single file to a known location, securely, with a single command. FTP isn't the most efficient way to accomplish this.

Fortunately, there's an alternative: SCP, the secure equivalent of cp, which also just happens to operate over a network. It can be used to copy a file to another local file securely, but its primary purpose these days is as a secure, non-interactive, and scriptable equivalent to FTP. It operates over the same TCP/IP channel as SSH, too, so all you need is an SSH-capable server in order to use it.

NOTE: Because SSH is fundamentally an authenticated application, so is SCP; there is no equivalent of anonymous FTP in the SCP world. But that's fine because in anonymous FTP there's no password to sniff anyway.

SCP isn't an application environment like FTP is; it has no command line of its own. Rather, you specify the file you want to get or put right at the command line, using a syntax like this:

```
Silver:~ btiemann$ scp btiemann@example.com:
➥/path/to/archive.zip .
stty: stdin isn't a terminal
archive.zip                    100% 529314    5.2KB/s
  00:00
```

Preceding the colon is a remote hostname and username combination, similar to how it's used in SSH. (As with SSH, if the username matches on the local and remote machine, you can leave it off.)

The colon separates the server and login credentials from the path to the file you want and differentiates between a remote copy and a local one. If you leave out the colon, SCP will look for or create a file on the local machine rather than trying to log in to a remote one.

The preceding example gets a file from the remote host (example.com) and copies it to the current directory, after authenticating your login just as in SSH. To send a file from your local machine to another host, reverse the last two arguments:

```
Silver:~ btiemann$ scp archive.zip
  btiemann@example.com:
```

If you omit the path following the colon on the remote server, SCP will place the file in the default login directory, which is your Home directory on the server.

You can even use SCP to transfer files from one remote location to another:

```
Silver:~ btiemann$ scp btiemann@myhost.com:
  archive.zip btiemann@example.com:
```

The drawback to SCP is that you have to know what the exact path and filename is that you want to send or receive before you invoke the command; there's no logging in, no browsing, and no directory manipulation (although you can use wildcards to match multiple files). The idea is that you use SSH to find out the path and filename you want, and then use SCP to perform the actual transfer. It's a little cumbersome this way, but hey—it's encrypted!

Download Web Files Using curl

```
curl http://remote_host/path/to/file
```

One final command-line utility to mention is one that fills in the blanks of today's too-full-featured-for-their-own-good web browsers: curl. This little bundle of usefulness takes a URL and downloads its targeted file directly to your desktop (or whatever folder you launch it from), without having to go through the rigmarole of loading it in your browser's handler and then trying to save it using whatever tools the handler may or may not provide. Suppose, for example, that you want to download a movie file, http://www.example.com/movies/Monkey.mov. Do you want to open it up in Safari, wait for it to launch the embedded QuickTime player, stop it automatically playing (and disturbing your co-workers with its soundtrack), poke around looking for a Save As function, and possibly not finding one (because the file has been saved in such a way that prevents saving)? I don't think so! curl to the rescue!

```
Silver:~ btiemann$ curl -O http://www.example.com/
➥movies/Monkey.mov
% Total    % Received % Xferd  Average Speed   Time
➥Time      Time  Current
                                 Dload  Upload
  Total
➥Spent    Left  Speed
100 4610k  100 4610k    0      0   701k      0
0:00:06
➥0:00:06 --:--:--  667k
```

You'll find that the file has been saved to the local directory and can now be opened in a separate application—all in one step. The -O option tells curl to send the downloaded output to a file with the same name as it had on the server. You can also use -o *filename* to specify a different filename.

This is a must-have tool for anyone who works with multimedia or web design files such as JavaScript or CSS include files, which sometimes cause full-featured browsers to trip up if you try to open them directly for download, when all you really want to do is fetch the file and save it. As you can see by reading its `man` page, `curl` does a lot more than just this—but it's its most popular use, and ample reason for the discerning Mac geek to know it's there.

Conclusion

Mac OS X may well be the world's most advanced operating system, as Steve Jobs is so fond of claiming, but that doesn't mean it has evolved beyond the necessity for an agile handling of the same basic tools and techniques that hard-core Unix users have sworn by for the past three decades. Indeed, an operating system that eschews such tools can hardly be said to be "advanced" at all. More than anything else, it's Apple's respectful and well-considered treatment of these raw building blocks right alongside its crowning GUI jewels that has made Mac OS X so popular among the high-tech creative community: the programmers, the system administrators, the web designers, and the Unix-heads who want the best of both worlds, the old and the new. No other operating system is even in the position to present a solid offering on both sides of the fence; the fact that Apple both *can* do so and *does* represents a large part of why it has come back from the brink to be one of the coolest technology companies to root for in the modern age.

Index

E - F

How can we make this index more useful? Email us at indexes@samspublishing.com

How can we make this index more useful? Email us at indexes@samspublishing.com

listing 287

M

BOOKS ONLINE

ENABLED

THIS BOOK IS SAFARI ENABLED

INCLUDES FREE 45-DAY ACCESS TO THE ONLINE EDITION

The Safari® Enabled icon on the cover of your favorite technology book means the book is available through Safari Bookshelf. When you buy this book, you get free access to the online edition for 45 days.

Safari Bookshelf is an electronic reference library that lets you easily search thousands of technical books, find code samples, download chapters, and access technical information whenever and wherever you need it.

TO GAIN 45-DAY SAFARI ENABLED ACCESS TO THIS BOOK:

● Go to **http://www.samspublishing.com/safarienabled**

● Complete the brief registration form

● Enter the coupon code found in the front of this book on page iii

If you have difficulty registering on Safari Bookshelf or accessing the online edition, please e-mail customer-service@safaribooksonline.com.